1718. 1896.

THE

STORY OF ALGIERS,

....NOW....

Fifth District of New Orleans.

The Past and the Present,

....BY....

WM. H. SEYMOUR.

LIMITED EDITION

ALGIERS DEMOCRAT PUBLISHING CO., LTD.

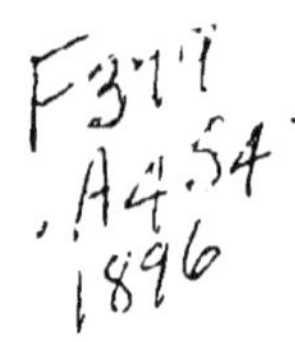

PREFACE.

These reminiscences of the past it has seemed to me a duty to record. An actor therein, circumstances afforded me exceptional advantages for a better view. I have, in many cases, been a witness to the facts alleged, or have obtained them from reliable sources.

The story extends from French Bienville to American Claiborne and thence to the present day. Commencing from the period when superstition cast a weird veil of mystery over the great river which surrounds us, and Indian legends peopled every nook of the section with fantastic creations of untutored fancy. Jesuit and Cavalier, Frenchman and Spaniard, Canadian and Yankee, natives of all climes, in our early day, intrigued and planned on this soil. What wonder, after this record, that it is so richly varied, so charming, so unique? History simply repeats itself as sound moves in waves.

I have confined my story, and not attempted, for fear of tiring the reader, to relate every incident of the past. It has been written after many a weary days' duties have ceased, when the residents of our busy district were in slumber. If the perusal of these pages proves of interest to the reader, then may I hope the story and other data have not been given in vain.

WM. H. SEYMOUR.

The Story of Algiers.

THIS town, known by its corporate title as the Fifth district of New Orleans, is a part of all that portion of the parish of Orleans on the right bank of the Mississippi river, commencing at the parish line of Jefferson, has a front upon the river of thirteen and a half miles, to within a short distance of the English turn by a depth of about three miles.

Comprised within that area are also included the towns of McDonogh and Tunisburg, several sugar plantations, many orange groves, cultivated gardens, dry docks, two railroads, one of which, with its connections, ends with the Golden Gate of the far away Pacific coast, evidencing truly that "westward the course of empire takes its way." The entire district has a population exceeding 16,000 people.

As a place of residence Algiers is most delightfully situated within a narrow elbow of the river, which makes the wide crescent on the city side. It has, therefore, a freer sweep of the air than the most famous localities of New Orleans. It is cooler and purer in atmosphere than in the city.

The first authentic reference to the place is by Le Page du Pratz, probably the earliest historian of our State, who was superintendent of the Kings plantation in 1718, by appointment of Louis, King of France, the tract embraced all land from the fort at Plaquemines to the Indian village of Chetimachas (now Donaldsonville), thence to Fort Rosalie, now the cite of Natchez, the section alluded to bearing at one time the name, also, of the "Company's Plantation." Rice, corn and indigo were raised for account of the company, and even exportation to the Spanish garrison at Pensacola. Eventually the laborers, African negroes, were all disposed of to planters on the German coast, now known as St. James and St. Charles parishes.

History, traditions and romance tell us that Bienville found the Indian village of Tchou-Tchouma, in 1718, where the Bayou St. John bridge is now located. Years pass on. The Baron Carondelet, Spanish governor of the provinces, selected his country house near the present corner of Carondelet street and the Delord plantation line, whilst his good dame, le baronne, planted her roses a block further back. Etienne de Bore and the Jesuit fathers cultivated about the same period, 1794, their sugar cane, and planted their oaks upon the ground where Farragut, Grant and Banks, one April day rested their forces in 1863. Later on, a little over a a score of years, and we behold upon the spot a cotton centennial exposition, with tributes from all portions of the globe, and view with reverence the old Liberty Bell of 1776. A new St. Charles hotel has arisen for the third time upon the identical spot where old Mr. Percy planted his vegetables in 1800, for consumption in the vieux carre, below the canal, which was subsequently filled, now the most charming boulevard of the South.

Our city journals sometime past gave an interesting account of the electri

WM. M. RAILEY,	GEO. S. KAUSLER,	ALLEN MEHLE,
President.	Vice President.	Sec. and Treas.

WM. M. RAILEY & CO.,

(*LIMITED*,)

Fire and Marine Insurance,

New No. 307 CARONDELET STREET,

REPRESENTING:

Phœnix Insurance Co., of Hartford, Conn., -	$ 5,588,058
Royal Insurance Co., of Liverpool, - -	43,000,000
Scottish Union and National, of Edinburgh, -	21,723,500
Lion Insurance Co., (Ltd.) of London, -	1,203,355
Marine Insurance Co., (Ltd.) of London, -	5,485,065
Sea Insurance Co., (Ltd.) of Liverpool, -	3,184,676

LOSSES EQUITABLY ADJUSTED AND PROMPTLY PAID.

GEO. HERBERT,

209 Olivier Street. Algiers Representative.

All these Companies were largely interested in the Algiers Fire, and Paid their Losses Promptly.

DWELLINGS ESPECIALLY SOLICITED.

power-house just completed on Marigny and Chartres street, but lovers of the old hallowed memories of the past have not forgotten that upon the same identical site, just a century ago, stood the old mansion of Marigny de Mandeville, who had for years, as his guest, Louis Phillippe, son of the duke of Orleans. Young Louis becoming in later years King of France, and the wealthiest man in all Europe. Marigny sleeps here in the old cathedral he loved so well, at the foot of the altar of "Our Lady of Lourdes," Louis, with his ancestors, at the Cathedral of St. Denis, in France. What a theme for thought, royalty is brushed aside, the new power of electricity in its place. It removes the ancient landmark, obliterates the last traces of ancient power and grandeur in Orleans island, making all things bend to its potent will.

But we are wandering from our subject. The town and district across the river Mechacebe, the red man's sacred stream is not as interesting, still there is matter from the traditions of the past. After the departure of le Page du Pratz homewards in 1734, the site seemed to drop into obscurity and but little is known. The great river rolled on to the Mexican gulf; the alligators slept indolently in the sun, while the pelican wandered in the lowland and dense cypress surroundings. The century waned, and in 1762, the Spanish regime became dominant through the cession from Louis XV, of the province, to Spain at Fountainebleau, of all the country known as Louisiana. On August 18, 1769, Don Alexander O'Reilly arrived in New Orleans with authority to receive possession of the province, no resistance was made, and on that day at 3 o'clock, at the place d'armes, the French flag was lowered, that of Spain unfurled and the government passed from the French to the Spanish authorities.

The cabildo met on December 1, under the presidency of O'Reilly and laws were enacted for the government, amongst others, for the sale of lands belonging to the crown, and the governor general required at stated times to contract with suitable persons styled "pobladores" to colonize the unsettled lands under his control.

Under these regulations, a large portion of the tract by royal patent, embracing all lands between the present line of Verret street and the upper line, now McDonogh, was granted to Louis Borepo, February 3, 1770, through whose title it finally passed to Bartholomi Duverje, for $18,000, on the 9th of August, 1805, and eventually became the original town of Algiers, meeting the same fate to a considerable extent upon the 20th of October, 1895, as befell its larger neighbor across the river, when a Franco-Spanish city, on the 8th of December, 1794, "when a strong north wind was blowing, and in three hours 212 dwellings and stores in the heart of town were destroyed," The old historical mansion in Algiers, used for many years as a temple of justice, and known in the olden times as the "Duverje house," the counterpart of which was the Louisiana State building, at the Columbia exposition of 1893, perished likewise in the flames with some hundreds of buildings in that section.

From the rapid reconstruction now progressing upon the tract, another year the ashes and ruins will have disappeared, a new town will have arisen like the Phœnix of old, and the sad memories of deprivations of homes and all that was dear will be a thing of the past.

Under the territorial government of Louisiana the right bank, under the legislative enactment of 1805, was a portion of the county of Orleans, which in [illegible] also Plaquemines and St. Bernard, same was under the jurisdiction of a [illegible]

DUVERJE PLANTATION HOME, ERECTED 1812.
(Subsequently the court house, destroyed by fire Oct. 20, 1895.)

which provided for its local government, until the annexation to the city by legislative act approved March 14, 1870, when all that portion of the parish on the right bank of the river became the fifth municipal district of the city of New Orleans.

Close by the river bank for many a year stood the somber dwelling of the philanthropist whose name is remembered now in stately school edifices throughout our fair city. Within its walls the owner for twenty-two long years toiled, reflected and pondered in composing that famous will, wherein his estate of millions was to accumulate perpetually for future posterity and the glory of his name, the full intent of which testament bearing date of 29th December, 1838, was so contrary to the jurisprudence of our civil law, that finally it went to Coin-Delisle, Giraud Marcade and other noted French jurists, advocates of the "Cour de Cassation" at Paris, who, on December 18, 1851, failed to reconcile its analogy to the Code of Napoleon, upon which our civil law is founded, wherein all bequests in the nature of fidei commissa are prohibited. The subsequent litigation upon the vast estate, divided between New Orleans and Baltimore, McDonogh's birthplace, would be too tedious to dwell upon.

Down the river to the right still stands intact, with the plantation surroundings, the Cazelar house, the headquarters of General Morgan, upon the 8th of January, 1815. Victory prevailed at Chalmette, vis a vis, but the glory of that event was partially dimmed by the flight of Morgan and his troops, who fled to Algiers, warmly pursued by the British forces. It was in this action that the British acquired the small flag, which now hangs amid the trophies of other wars in Whitehall, London, with this inscription: "Taken at the battle of New Orleans." Upon one of the guns captured at Cazelars, the victors read: "Taken at the surrender of Yorktown, 1781."

Before reaching the old plantation alluded to one meets the little hamlet of Tunisburg. Close by there, old residents still point out where stood until a few years ago a picturesque cottage, but now crumbled into decay. This was formerly the home of W. B. Howell, father-in-law of Jefferson Davis, to whom it was sold on the 3rd of January, 1853. Mr. Davis spent many pleasant days at the old home when his busy life permitted. Eventually the property was sold under the confiscation act of Congress, in 1865. After the demise of Mr. Davis, suit was instituted in our courts in 1892. The writer appeared for the defendant, who had only acquired by the purchase the life interest of Mr. Davis therein, acknowledging the correctness of the claim for restitution. Judge Monroe never had a pleasanter judicial duty assigned him than that of restoring to Mrs. Varina Howell Davis, as widow, her community half in the old property of her father; to Miss Varina Davis and Mrs. Margaret Howell Hayes, the residue, as the sole heirs of Jefferson Davis, their father, to whom in said proportions the property still belongs.

Within the borders of the subject of this sketch many incidents of the past can be related. 'Twas here that Raphael Semmes assumed command of the Sumter on the 22d of April, 1861. On the 3d of June ensuing, he formally placed the vessel in commission. On that day the colors were hoisted for the first time of the Southern Confederacy. The vessel was then lying in the stream off Lavergne street. These identical colors were by him subsequently transferred to the Alabama, going down with the latter in the engagement with the Kearsarge at Cherbourg, France, on Sunday, June 19, 1864. By the cruel irony of fate, the last flag of the same service disappeared with the Webb, when destroyed by her crew to prevent capture by the Federal ships within sight of the lower part of the district

THE
PHOTO ENG
CO. N.O.

Semmes first threw his colors to the southern breeze.

A handsome edifie for educational purposes has just been completed by the city authorities, and baptized "Belleville," upon the grounds where stood for many years the old Hughes Hotel. Truth again proves stranger than fiction. Upon the same spot, on January 30, 1861, Captain John G. Breshwood, master of the revenue cutter McClelland, while visiting the Hughes, his vessel being at the time at anchor in the stream off Belleville street, was handed a dispatch just received from Secretary John A. Dix, of the treasury at Washington, sent by the latter in a moment of inspiration, a heroic sentiment, which concluded, "If any one attempts to haul down the American flag, shoot him on the spot," which, copied and recopied through the press of the North, flew like wild-fire from lip to lip, like a tocsin or trumpet peal.

The Algerians have had many pleasant people at times to cast their lot among them. Albert Delpit, the charming writer, long a resident of France, is "native here, and to the manner born," while Ruth McEnery Stuart, one of Louisiana's fair daughters, passed from girlhood to womanhood amongst us, dreaming and weaving, perhaps, in thought, those of "The Golden Wedding" and "Christmas Gifts" to come in future days.

Minister Pitkin, to the Argentine Republic, also refers with pleasure to the period when he likewise had his cottage home here, facing the broad river, encircled with rose vines and the stately magnolia, in close proximity to the McDonogh home.

The theme chosen is a lengthy one, and will end with the origin of the name Algiers. Many, many stories have been written and foisted upon the public on the subject, reaching back to the early part of the century. Several of the old citizens have preserved the traditions and stories of the past.

The powder magazine of the French regime and subsequently of the Spanish according to the ancient maps, several being still extant, shows that the location was at the head of rue de la Poudriere, or Powder street, a portion of which street adjoins the Grand Isle Depot; the balance having long since been submerged by caving banks. Stoddard, in his early sketches of Louisiana, 1812, tells us that it faced the government house, on the corner of Toulouse street and the levee; "that a guard was always stationed there and generally relieved weekly." An old citizen, Llulla, by name, long since gathered to his fathers, related oft' that the name was suggested by one of O'Reilly's soldiers, who had returned here after the expedition which Spain undertook against Algeria, where they were so badly repulsed. This old soldier, after several years absence, returned to Louisiana and found the magazine surrounded by a hamlet of a dozen houses, still without a name, with the guardians of Carondelet still in possession. From the old son of Castile and Leon, far from the flow of the Guadalquivir, at his suggestion the name was given, which has held so tenaciously; still stranger to relate, not another town bearing a like appellation is to be found throughout our broad land.

Thus it came from the far away colonial white-walled city in a province of France, upon whose shores the blue waters of the Mediterranean sparkle in the bright sunlight, whose breezes bear afar the sweet odor of the olive and myrtle.

THE
PHOTO·
ENG·CO·
N.O.

Chronological, Historical Notes and Sketches.

On the 6th of April, 1682, the Sieur de la Salle and companions, who descended from Canada by way of the lakes and river, at last reached the gulf after their long and perilous voyage upon the Meschaebe. Three days ensuing they ascended the river, and upon the right bank erected a column and a cross. The arms of France were attached to the column with this inscription, "Louis, the Great King of France and Navarre Reigns, the 9th of April, 1682." Thus taking possession of the whole country of Louisiana, then extending from the gulf to Canada, for the French King, the nation and people contained therein, the seas and all the streams flowing into the grand river, which la Salle named St. Louis. From this acquisition to the crown of France, twenty States have been since formed as part of the Federal Union. Two score miles in a direct line from Algiers, at this epoch, brings one to the site where the King's cross was erected, proclamation and proces verbal, signed and registered by Metairie, the royal notary, commissioned to accompany the discoverors; the ceremony being concluded with religious songs and cries of "Vive le Roi."

The first sketch showing the site of this town was drawn by M. De Serigay, in the year 1710, and is still extant in the Depot des Cartes Marine a Paris. The buildings shown were the powder magazines, about Bouny and Morgan streets of present day.

A plan of the city and suburbs, including the right bank, drawn in 1815, a certified copy of which is on file in the Department of the Interior at Washington, shows the Duverje, Verret and Le Beuf plantation residences. A French traveler whose work is in the library Bibliotheque Nationale, Paris, writes that in departing from New Orleans, January 5th, 1817, "their vessel hoisted sails opposite the Duverje plantation home, just above the powder magazines, and a short distance below the slaughter pens, or abattoir of that period, about Olivier street.

The first shipyard with marine ways was established in 1810, by Andre Seguin, a native of Havre, France, at the head of the street which stills bears his name, facing the office where the Algiers Democrat is now established. The site was purchased from Mrs. Duverje, being the first piece of property sold by her from the original Duverje plantation.

Verret's canal was excavated in 1814, by Furcy Verret. The canal was used by Lafitte, Dominique You and other corsairs of the gulf, for passage of their small vessels to Cheniere Cammada, Grande Terre and Barataria, where their settlements were located. At the head site of the canal may yet be seen a brick wall upon the adjoining site, formerly stood a square redoubt. The historian, Latour, tells us, "The redoubt was furnished wish a small powder magazine, and was mounted with two twenty-four pounders. Its battery commanded at once the road and the river under command of Captain Henley." It was near here that Mor[illegible] troops rallied after their flight on the 8th of January, 1815.

Belleville Foundry was commenced in 1846. Front walls, still in existence, were designed after the Penrhynn Castle in Wales. During 1861, occupied [illegible] Federal, and subsequently as a Confederate prison, destroyed by fire.

Captain Morse's residence, corner Belleville and Alix streets, was ori[illegible]

The
Photo Eng
Co N O

that of W. H. Brown, who was killed by the explosion of the Louisiana at Canal street wharf, the 15th of November, 1849, upon which occasion so many perished.

The old sugar-house on one of Camus' plantations is still in existence, the building, a brick one, was erected in 1795, while Louisiana was under Spanish rule. It was at that period that the manufacturing of sugar was successfully introduced in the State, and demonstrated to be practicable, and thus began a source of ever growing wealth. The machinery of those days was exceedingly simple; steam has superceded the patient mule; bisulphates and other chemicals have taken away pure lime, then used, but all of the modern innovations fail in comparison to the purity and sweetness of the product of the olden times.

Mitchell & Co. published in 1840 the New Orleans Directory. The names of all white male citizens who then resided in Algiers, McDonogh and Tunisburg are therein given.

McDonogh's home was situated in the square bounded by Adams, Jefferson, Jackson and Homer streets. The site is submerged at high water every season. His tomb is located in the cemetery, just beyond the parish line, upon the continuation of Valette street. It is well worthy of inspection to the curious-seekers.

Verret's sugar-house was situated, for many a year, upon the present site of the Morgan roundhouse.

The race track was outside of Opelousas, vis-a-vis to the Duverne cemetery. The entrance was at the corner of Alix and Bouny. Bob Nicholson was gate keeper.

Where engine fire company No. 17 is now located on Delaronde, near Bouny street, was the parish courthouse for many years, until the removal to the present site in the spring of 186[illegible]. In front of Mrs. Norton's dwelling, on Olivier, near Alix, may yet be seen the roots of a large oak tree. This is the identical spot where the midnight meetings of the voudous, and celebration on St. John eve annually took place, the negro worshipers, with their orgies and invocations, chanting in their frenzy, "Aie! Aie! Voudoo Magnan!" "Eh! eh! Bomba houe."

Opelousas Hotel was a brick building at the corner of Pelican and Verret streets, A. de Monasterio, owner; constructed in 1850; occupied by Colonel Stephen Thomas and the Eighth Regiment of Vermont Volunteers; destroyed while so occupied by fire, August, 1862. Colonel Thomas was subsequently elected governor upon his return to Vermont. The de Monasterios have never been paid for their loss, although the claim has been on file for many years with the Spanish minister at Washington. Attakapas Hotel, subsequently Wilson House, built in 1838, destroyed by fire, upon the site now occupied by Borne's shop, Patterson street. The Willow Grove Hotel, situated some two blocks above Morgan street, all of the site and adjoining ground caved in the river on the 30th of May, 1844.

On February 17th, 1849, Jean B. Dupiere sold to the United States government, for the site of a navy yard, real estate below Algiers for $15,000. By expropriation proceedings in the Federal Courts, in May, 1894, additional ground was attained from the Oliviers for $37,000 and the Trepagniers for $7500.

The St. Charles Hall, on Patterson street, built for A. L. Hasling, was for many years the only ball room in town, and was the scene of many a social festive and political gathering. It was also used for amateur theatrical purposes from 1874 to 1878 by the Algiers Dramatic Association, the officers of which were: A. B. Seger, president; Louis F. Chalin, treasurer; W. H. Seymour, stage manager;

G. W. Dunbar's Sons,

NEW ORLEANS, LA.,

STANDARD FRUIT SYRUPS,

In Every Variety.

Orgeat,		Pineapple,
Raspberry,		Vanilla,
Lemon,		Strawberry,
Gooseberry,		Ginger,
Orange,		Blackberry,
Sarsaparilla,		Banana,
Rose,		Raspberry,
Ginger,	Natural,	Vinegar.

Our establishment is thoroughly organized for the manufacture of the various Fruit Syrups, whose purity and excellence are acknowledged. The genuine article has our Name and Trade Mark on the Label, Cap and Cork.

SOLD BY ALL FANCY GROCERS.

WHAT WE DO:

We give you a Carpet in Brussels, Velvet, Moquette, Axminster or Wilton

AT LOWEST PRICES,

and make and lay with Lining without charge. You have not two or three samples, but a full line of the

Most Desirable Patterns

to select from, many our private designs. It is the same with **MATTING,** in all grades from 10c up. The very best made at 35 cents. Our's line is above comparison

MIOTO RUGS,

All Sizes, Just Received. They Speak For Themselves.

Think of Us. Ask Your Friends, and They Will Tell You to Go to

A. BROUSSEAU'S SON,

23-25 CHARTRES ST.

GLASSWARE.

BAR GOODS.

CORKS.

H. LOUBAT,

AGENT,

IMPORTER AND DEALER IN

BOTTLES,

Bottle Caps, Labels,

Sealing Wax, Etc.,

512, 514 and 516 BIENVILLE STREET,

Near Decatur,

NEW ORLEANS, LA.

TELEPHONE 1372.

Miss Myra Gerard, musical directoress; J. F. DeSeames, scenic artist. Many delightful plays were rendered, with one exception, that of September 14th, 1874. The male members of the association contributing to a more serious drama, being enacted upon the levee at Liberty place where the monument now stands.

During the late conflagration was destroyed a queer, curious, old fashioned two-story building, erected by A. L. Hasling, at 68 Delaronde street, long occupied by an odd lot of tenants. At one time Laura D. Fair-Greyson resided there. She went to California, and is the same woman who assasinated Alexander P Crittenden, a noted lawyer, on the steamer El Capitan, all of which became a cause celebre owing to the prominence of the parties. This was on the 3d of November, 1870.

A. B. Bacon was editor and publisher of the Algiers Newsboy in 1860, at the corner of Morgan and Bermuda streets. For what was considered as a disloyal article published in the paper in 1862 same was suppressed, and Mr. Bacon incarcerated at Fort Jackson by order of General Butler. William Teal-Bensick and other citizens accompanied him for being disloyal to the Union.

Geo. W. Hopkins published from Morgan street the Algiers Weekly News, a small single sheet paper, during 1864 66. This was succeeded by the Algiers Independent, Wm. H. Toy, editor and publisher. The Independent was well edited, and became quite popular in Algiers. During 1868-70 Mr. Toy was printer, editor, devil and publisher all at one time.

The latter journal in time was succeeded by the Peoples' Advocate, Lawrence and Givens, publishers, and eventually by W. R. Lawrence only, 1888-90. After this the Algiers Democrat, published by the Algiers Democrat Publishing Co., Limited, whereof Martin Behrman is president and C. M. Jennings, secretary, the latter being editor also; the first issue was published in September, 1894. The above enumerated are the only journals that were ever actually printed and published on the right bank of the river.

The Legislature, by enactment, at the session held February, 1827, gave exclusive privileges to Auguste Coycault and Bazile Gosselin to establish and maintain a steam ferry-boat to the opposite side of the river. Cabin arrangements were to be provided for at least twenty passengers; the rates were fixed at one bit for a foot passenger and fifty cents for a horse.

St Bartholomew's church was erected upon the site where Guillaud's furniture store was established, facing the courthouse. Mrs. Octavie Duverje donated the ground for church purposes only, on the 10th of December, 1848, Bishop Antoine Blanc accepting. The edifice was dismantled in 1872, thereby the donation became void, the real estate reverted back to the heirs of Mrs. Duverje. By a decree of court rendered against the Catholic archbishop, N. J. Perche, on the 6th of March, 1883, the property was sold at auction April 14th, 1883, and Louis Guillaud became the purchaser for $1725. The Church of the Holy Name of Mary, on Verret street, is the successor to St. Bartholomew's Church, of Algiers, and a noble successor it is.

Jacques Villere and Thomas Urquhart were the delegates to the first constitutional convention held in this State, 1812.

Charles J. Villere was the Whig delegate to form the Constitution of 1852.

George W. Lewis was delegate to the convention of 1861, and was one of the seventeen delegates who voted against the secession of the States from the Union. Wm. H. Seymour was the Union delegate chosen in 1864, being the youngest member of

E W Foster

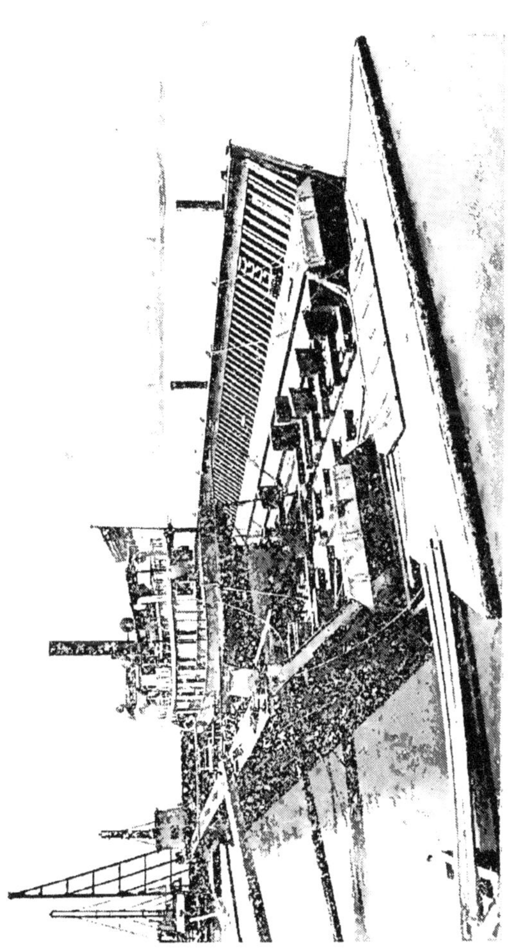

the convention. Stephen B. Packard, 1878, and Wm. Francis Loan in 187[illegible], were the respective Republican delegates elected to the convention of those years.

Arthur Fortier was the first justice of the peace and president of the police jury. He presided from 1838 to 1862, with the exception of one term, filled by James Aikman. The first suit filed in the magistrate's court was on the 27th of July, 1838, plaintiff was Charlotte Irma Latour, the defendants Harrold and Hughes. The case was appealed to the City Court of New Orleans, J. N. Duncan, judge, and affirmed for plaintiff. Suit was for $115 for the services of a slave named Tom. Charles W. Morse was the first constable of the court.

Prior to 1840 this portion of the parish was under the jurisdiction of a police jury, which embraced the entire Parish of Orleans. Casimer Lacoste was the first member to represent Orleans right bank on the Jury. On the 28th of March, 1840, the Legislature created a separate Police Jury for all that portion upon the right bank. The Governor appointed as members thereof: Furcy Verret, Casimer Lacoste, Jean B. Olivier, Edward Fazendé and Caliste Villere. In 1855 the Legislature enlarged their power and jurisdiction. Wm H. Seymour was the last president, having filled the position for five years by election until 1870.

The act of 1840 was amended in 1855, the Legislature enlarging their power and jurisdiction. This last act, with subsequent amendments, was the local governing power, until the annexation to the City of New Orleans on the 16th of March, 1870, becoming thereby the Fifth Municipal District.

Under the territorial government of Louisiana the right bank, under the legislative enactments of 1805, was a portion of the county of Orleans, which included also Plaquemines and St. Bernard.

The first regatta took place on Sunday, June 30, 1840, opposite the Willow Grove Hotel. It was a row boat race, and the prize was an elegant liquor stand, and resulted in a victory for the Water Witch. In 1843 there was another race between the Algerine and the Lady of Lyons clubs, the prize, a silk flag, was awarded to the latter club. This was the last race for many years.

The Mississippi, in the spring of 1844, began to rise early and rapidly. About the 1st of May tha water began to decrease. On the 30th of May the bank above the point caved in, carrying with it a number of small shanties and sheds and some cotton. Below this spot stood the boathouses, a produce store and a tavern, but no one for a moment supposed that these buildings were in danger. The evil was thought to be past, but that evening about half-past nine, while many of the residents were at church, the alarm was sounded that the whole point was going down into the river. In an instant the church was deserted; all flocked to the river just in time to see the roof of the old warehouse whirled away by the angry, seething flood into the darkness of the stormy night.

When the morning broke not a vestage of the boathouses or the buildings near them remained, and on the spot where they had stood the lead found nine fathoms of water.

Nothing in any of the buildings was saved, except a canary in its cage, which was rescued from the Algerine boathouse by Mr. Clark, one of the club. In the Lady of Lyons boathouse was a new raceboat, the "Claude Melnotte," and a number of prizes, all of which were lost. So the great Father of Waters struck the death blow to the rowing interests of our city, and after being successfully practiced for nearly ten years, rowing for pleasure became a thing of the past about our shores.

So it remained until the spring of 1869, when one April day a little white yawl

was launched on the old Bayou St. John, in which was the members of a new era. The inauguration of the St. John Club the formation of the Pelican Club, and subsequently of the Orleans Riversides and Howards, brings us down to the celebrated regatta of September 14th, 1874, which occurred at Carrollton at the same minute that the bloody conflict was going on between the Metropolitan police and citizens on the levee, was followed almost immediately by the dissolution of the Louisiana State Rowing Association, under whose auspices it was given.

More landslides took place in the river. During the year 1867 a marine wavs with a schooner thereon was lost, and the loss of the Grand Isle depot during the summer of 1894, is still fresh in our memory, all of which was in close proximity to that sustained by the owners of the Willow Grove hotel on the memorable 30th of May, 1844, half a century previous.

The United States Marine Hospital.

This hospital was situated at McDonogh, just above the parish line in Jefferson, and occupied a square, measuring three hundred and fifty feet each way, which was enclosed by a good substantial fence. The edifice measured in front one hundred and sixty feet, by seventy-eight feet deep, from the side of which two adjuncts extended fifty feet further back, leaving sufficient room between them for a spacious court, immediately behind the centre of the main building.

The whole building was laid off into three stories. It was fifty feet from the ground to the eaves, and one hundred and thirty-five feet to the top of the flag-staff, which surmounted the belvidere. It was built in the Gothic style; it was commenced in 1834, but many years elapsed before final completion; when finished, the total cost was $130,000; it would accommodate two hundred and sixty-nine persons. The grounds laid out were embellished with shrubbery. As seen from the Mississippi river, or from the city front, the structure presented a very majestic appearance. It stood in a healthy position, elevated and dry, and from its great heighth commanded a complete view of the river, city, surrounding country and a whole forest of masts from the sailing vessels on the city side, affording at once a delightful and a busy prospect that must have had a great tendency to cheer the hours of the convalescent within its walls.

After the secession of Louisiana from the Union, the buildings were taken possession of by the government officers, or provost marshal of the Confederates. In the grounds adjoining was established powder magazines. An explosion occurred there during the night time, towards the close of December, 1861, which was heard for miles around, and the entire edifices on the ground entirely destroyed.

The New Orleans, Opelousas and Great Western Railroad Company, Now Morgan, Louisiana and Texas Railroad.

This railroad was incorporated by the legislature during the session of 1853, by an act approved April 22d of that year, under the No. 140, for the purpose of constructing a railroad from the town of Algiers to some point on the Sabine river, the boundary between Louisiana and Texas. The commissioners from Algiers

Z. W. TINKER,
President.

F. H. MITCHELL,
Sec. and Treas.

INCORPORATED JUNE 1894.

SECURITY BREWING COMPANY,

Successors Algiers Brewing Company.

FIFTH DISTRICT, NEW ORLEANS, LA.,

General Offices and City Depot :

341, 343, 345 N. DIAMOND ST.,

Opposite St. Mary's Market.

MANUFACTURERS OF THE CELEBRATED

Imperial Lager Beer,

THE FINEST BEER IN THE SOUTH.

were J. W. Stanton, R. F. Nichols, Leon Bernard, R. B. Sumner, John Hughes, J. B. Olivier, A. B. Seger and J. Thayer. The parish of Orleans, right bank, by vote of the tax payers and ordinances of the Police Jury, subscribed $75 000 to assist in the construction of the road. In the course of time every dollar was paid.

The first office of the company was for several years at No. 75 Exchange place, near Bienville street. The first officers were Wm. G. Hewes, president; A. B. Seger, vice president; B. F. Flanders, secretary. In 1856, trains ran only to Tigerville, a distance of 66 miles, leaving the depot at Algiers every day at 8:30 a. m., arriving at their destination at 12:10 p. m. The fare each way was $2.50.

The office of the company was removed to the Pontalba building, corner of St. Peter and Decatur streets about 1859. After the city was captured by Farragut and Butler had assumed command, Captain A. W. Morse of the Federal forces was placed in full control of the entire road during May, 1862, and so remained until February, 1866, when all was restored to the company, by direction of the authorities at Washington. The company then established their office in the upper floor of the building corner of Canal and Decatur streets, with A. B. Seger, president; G. W. R. Bayley, superintendent; W. Squires, secretary, who continued as such for several years. When the road was returned to the company it was with impaired tracks, small rolling stock, ruined cross ties and bridges.

Large capital was required to rebuild and extend the road and the efforts to procure necessary means to pay matured interest on the bonds and to extend the road were utterly futile.

The bond holders instituted suit in the U. S. Court, and executory process issued. By virtue of the writ of seizure and sale directed to the U. S. Marshal the road was sold to Charles Morgan on the 5th of April, 1869, for $2.050.000, and on 31st of July, 1869, Mr. Morgan, having complied with all the conditions of the sale, the Marshal gave him title, and put him in possession of the lower portion of the original division of the road

At a sheriff's sale about the 22d day of April, 1870, under writs from the Seventh District Court, of Orleans parish, against said company, also from one issued by the Fourth District Court. Charles Morgan became the purchaser of the graded road, etc., belonging to the said company beyond Brashear, thus becoming the sole owner of all the road franchises and privileges formally belonging to the Opelousas Railroad Company.

Thus we have traversed the records bearing thereon. Mr. Morgan placed his son-in-law, C. A. Whitney and A. C. Hutchinson, an old officer of the former Company prior to the war, at Brashear City, as agents of the road, and George Pandely as superintendent. Messrs. Morgan and Whitney having died, Mr. Hutchinson became president of the Morgan, Louisiana and Texas Railroad and Steamship Company, successor to the old Opelousas Company; also manager of the Southern Pacific Company, Atlantic System.

The Southern Pacific Plant.

Few people have an idea of the magnitude of the plant of the Southern Pacific Company in the corporate limits of Algiers. Standing on the river front, one notices extensive sheds and wharves with ships lined up in front, and looking back into the rear a series of buildings loom up into view. This casual glance but faintly

CANAL STREET FERRY-HOUSE.

pictures the extent of the plant and the variety of industries which flourish within the lines of the company. Once within the great wharf, which stretches along the river front for a distance of nearly half a mile, one begins to wonder at its vastness; walking over to the depot and then to the many shops, each a separate plant in itself, the realization gradually dawns upon you that the square mile of territory covered by them contains enough to form a village of handsome proportions, and that it is not unlike the famous town ot Pullman, Ill., in many respects. Having seen as much as you could in walking through from one building to the other and accompanied by one familiar with all the details of the various departments, whose lucid explanations make clear all doubtfui subjects that come under observation, you come to the conclusion that what you have seen has been an actual revelation to you and one of a most agreeable sort, if you happen to be one who has the industrial interests of the city of New Orleans and vicinity at heart. It is the largest of its kind in the South.

It is a picture for a skeptic to look upon and be convinced that the railroads of this city are not always working against the interests of the city, and that they are not always trying to send the city to the "demnition bow-bows" to achieve their own welfare regardless of that of others, Corporations are generally credited with having no souls, but the manner in which affairs are conducted in this plant proves an exception. The feeling between the employer and employed is such as is seldom seen where 3000 or 4000 men are dependent on a great concern like this for their bread and butter. A sort of friendship seems to prevail among all. Things are run on a strictly business basis, however, but instead of this tending to promote discord, as is sometimes the result in big plants elsewhere, it has a contrary effect, the employees having the intelligence to appreciate the necessity for it, and knowing that it is for their interest, as well as that of the company, for if the company met with disaster they know full well that it would be an equal disaster for them, for, to tell the truth, it is the life of Algiers. It is like the heart of an animal- if it ceased to beat, if the great pulsations of the myriad hammer, saws and trucks ceased, it would be a blow from which Algiers would be many years recovering. Everybody in the town feels this, and says so without the slightest hesitation.

All the men employed here are residents of the place; many have been in the company's service from a quarter to a third of a century. The mighty influence of time has, therefore, had almost as much to do with the establishment of that spirit of harmony among the men and the employers as the policy of fairness and conciliation adopted by the latter. Many, through advancing years, have almost worn out in the service, but whose sons and grandsons are gradually taking their places, preference always being given them as new men are taken on. Promotions are made from employers only, and every man feels that with character, ability and loyalty it is only a question of time in his advancement.

Going down the river on the right bank, nearly a mile from the ferry landing, the first buildings of the road seen are the lumber sheds and yards, and then are several barn-like structures in which are stored yawls, boats, anchors, rope and tackle and other shipping paraphernalia. Then you reach the incline, with the bridge tower, where the transfer boats run in to discharge their bulky portable cargoes of freight cars, loaded or unloaded. This incline is a fine piece of mechanical work, being operated from the tower to suit the stage of the river, keeping the tracks flush with the level of those of the boats. Stretching along to the left, almost as far as the eye can reach, there are the great wharf sheds, while from the

The Photo Eng
Co N. Y.

street where you are standing the masts of the many steamers lying beside them loading and discharging their cargoes, rise to quite a height above the sheds. Right here is the great joint which connects the two systems of the Southern Pacific Company—the railroad whieh extends from New Orleans to the state of Oregon in the northwest, and the steamship lines, which run to New York and Central American ports and Havana.

To the right there extends the series of buildings which rise to different heights and dot the vast area at intervals for half a mile back. The first to attract attention is the old passenger depot, now used as a coach shed.

This is noticeable for its picturesqueness. The front and sides are covered with a close-clinging vine, which completely obscures the brick work, but it is kept constantly trimmed around the windows, while in bold relief stand out the words: "Southern Pacific Railroad, New Orleans to Portland, 3254 Miles," in gold letters forming a fine contrast to the dark green background. This is a spacious structure. filled with passenger coaches, sleepers, etc., and also contains several offices, including that of the division superintendent, and a large force of clerks are at work.

Then you strike the machine shops and foundry. This is a great brick building, where, during the busy season, the disciples of Vulcan hold high carnival and the music of the hammer and the anvil sounds from early morn till the fall of evening. The facilities are such that everything can be made from the finest steel spring to a locomotive ready for service. One of the features of this shop is a monster trip-hammer, worked by steam. which can pound an axle into shape in two minutes or split a hair, so fine is its mechacism and so massive. Another big piece of machinery is a lathe, which is the foundation of every machine shop, but this one is of the mastodon species and is used in turning and finishing the large steamship shafts, etc.

Here was seen the laying of the foundation, so to speak, for the building of locomotives. The forward and driving wheels were being placed in position. All the other parts which enter into its construction were strewn around, ready to be appropriately placed. On all sides were the usual other fittings of a machine shop only on a scale far larger than ordinarily exists elsewhere. Several tracks run into the place, some for the accommodation of trucks and locomotives to be repaired and built, and others for the moving of heavy work.

Another great building, several hundred feet long, and almost as wide, not far removed from the machine shops and foundry, is the carshop where passenger and sleeping coaches are repaired and built. It is practically a great shed, with several tracks running through it and open at both ends. Here was a mail car with half its side taken off, and around were a gang sawing and fitting the strips of poplar, while other were nailing them on. A little father on was a passenger coach on jackscrews, its trucks having been sent over to the machine shop to be rebuilt. Yonder was a car having a new roof put on, and so on throughout the shed. Among the appliances in use here are hydraulic jackscrews, devised by Foreman Hilderbrandt.

In another part of the yards you come to the paint shops, where the finishing touches are put on. Here the coaches are sand-papered and painted and varnished until their sides are smooth as glass and shine like burnished silver. There is also here in one of the departments a silver-plating plant, where all the silver-work on the coaches is renewed.

WILLIAM G. COYLE. CHARLES G. COYLE.

W. G. COYLE & CO.,

Coal and Towing.

TUG BOATS:	BRANCH YARDS:
B. D. Wood.	Baton Rouge, La.
Ella Andrews.	Plaquemine, La.
Mamie Coyle.	
Captain Chamberlain.	

Landing and Retail Yard:

COR. RIVER AND SLIDELL AVENUE.

A little walk brings you to the molding and planing mill, where all the lumber is put into shape for use. This is a large building divided into two floors, the lower one being devoted to the heavy work, and is fitted up with all the appurtenances of a full-fledged mill. There are planers of all sorts and sizes, saws, grooving machines, etc. Up stairs there are a variety of industries all hived together as a happy family. In one corner there is the upholsterer, who renews and makes cushions and mattresses for the sleeping cars and passenger coaches. Over in the opposite corner is the cabinet-maker, who does all the fine work on the furnishing of the cars. Then a short distance from him is another silver plating plant. Further on you come to a section devoted to the man whose business is to resilver plate-glass mirrors, with which all first-class coaches are sumptuously fitted. Then the entire center of the floor, taking up a space of 200 square feet, is divided into two sections, one on the lower side containing a quantity of steamship equipments, from an anchor to a dinner bell, and the other to a storehouse for patterns, of which there are said to be fully $50,000 worth. Over in another corner is the office of Draftsman Henning, who also has charge of the patterns. These patterns are of every conceivable piece of casting, car wheels, pulleys, axles, axle boxes and even to anchors. When any of these articles are wanted and they do not happen to be in stock, the pattern is sent down to the foundry and in a short time it is cast, finished off and ready for use. Mr. Henning has a force of subordinates, and under his care are preyared the plans for any piece of work which the company may desire, from a locomotive to a new car step

Still pursuing the journey through that hive of industry, for by this time you come to realize that you have undertaken a journey, you enter the roundhouse the huge stable where the locomotives are stalled, cleaned and given minor repairs and kept until necessity calls them out for a spin. In this division there are about sixty-five of the iron monsters, from the smallest switch engine to the imposing 60-ton passenger locomotives which annihilate space at the rate of sixty miles an hour. Foreman J. P. Nolan has the care of all of them.

On the way to the repair car shed you pass blacksmith shops, an oilhouse, where all the oil used on the road and ships is stored, and isolated from every other building, and a sandhouse, where the sand for the locomotives is dried out by a heating process and stored for use as the occasion requires. The repair car shed is an immense structure with 2000 feet of track under cover, and four deep. Here freight cars are made over by the hundreds, and when working the full force can be made at the rate of five a day, all-completed and painted. Parallel with this building is a platform where is stored all the iron work used in the construction and repair of these cars.

Away beyond is the lumber green, where all the rough lumber used in the different departments is stored away for future use. There is one other building which comes into view on the return trip to the river front, which had been overlooked. That is the general storehouse, where steamship supplies, tools, nails pulleys, and in fact all sorts of iron and wood work are kept. It is really a big hardware store, and there are clerks who furnish to anyone with the proper order from the superintendent any article desired. Up stairs is a large loft, where the steamers' sails are made and repaired

The journey back allows you to notice the vast area of ground covered by tracks, which, at this dull season of the year, are covered with empty freight cars,

the majority awaiting repairs, the freight repair shed being about the busiest portion of the grounds now.

Reaching the river front again, before entering the wharf sheds, you observe on the right three large buildings. These are devoted to the steamship lines. One is the storehouse where supplies, rope and tackles and other such articles are kept to supply immediate demands. Just adjoining is the steamship blacksmith and boiler shops and carpenter shed, and then is the boiler house, which supplies the steam for the various purposes needed on the wharf.

All these buildings so far described are of brick or iron, and of the best workmanship, planned and built by the employes of the company. A most noticeable feature of the whole thing is the absolute cleanliness which prevails everywhere. Every piece of machinery is as clean as a pin and shines like a new dollar, and even the floors would do credit to a well kept dwelling. The grounds and all the surroundings are in this condition, while here and there are bright groups of flowers, indicating so plainly that something besides mere labor is thought of, and that some one in the company's service has an eye to beauty.

Once on the wharf, Captain Morse, the superintendent, undertakes the courtesy of acting as guide, and all of the interesting facts are pointed out. To begin with, it might be stated that this wharf shed (for it is covered from one end to the other) is almost half a mile long, and on an average about a hundred feet wide. Standing at the upper end of it your range of vision will hardly reach to the other end. And what a sight it is when there are several ships loading and unloading at the same time! When working the full force on this wharf there are nearly a thousand men hustling and bustling and moving about trucking the masses of freight to and fro, and they look like bees in a hive.

At this end is the sugar shed, where the vessels from Havana tie up and unload their cargoes of Cuban sweetness during the sugar season on the Ever Faithful Isle. Here there are tracks cut into the wharf, and the floors of the cars are flush with it, so that the cars can be loaded almost from the ship's side. In this manner there is provision for loading forty cars at the same time. Right here it might be well to say something of the system of elevators in use in unloading ships. It is to be found nowhere else in the United States, except in New York, and has been in use in Algiers for the past fifteen years, where it has greatly facilitated the work. At intervals, corresponding to the various portholes of the ships, there are inclines in the wharf which are raised and lowered automatically to suit the stage of the water and the level of the portholes, and on one side of each of these inclines is an endless carrier running from the ship's side to the level of the wharf. These are operated by a lever, the speed being about that of a man on a slow trot. A man rolls his truck-load of freight from the ship's side onto the carrier, and is carried up to the wharf without the slightest exertion on his part, and when he reaches the top the truck rolls off and is given an impetus which permits him to roll it along the level without much waste of strength. These carriers are located for two ships' length along the wharf.

Passing on you come to the New York shed, and then to the Havana forwarding and receiving section, and then to the Central American section. The facilities are such that in a rush a ship can be loaded and unloaded at the same time without the slightest confusion. The men are all experienced in the work, and know their duties perfectly, and go about them with a system that is surprising to

an outsider, white and blacks working together in perfect harmony. Eight ships a week can be cared for when the occasion demands.

Further down the wharf, near the lower end, there is a sort of storehouse during the summer season, and still further the space is utilized as a carpenter shop. The shed is provided with every precaution against fire, there being a thorough system of hose running all through it, besides water barrels and extinguishers at intervals. Light is provided by electricity, the company owning their own equipment, but securing the current from the Algiers Ice and Electric Light Company.

Beyond the wharf is the shipyard, where the El Mozo was built, but at present it is but an empty space, there being no boats in course of construction. There are two boats lying up against the wharf, undergoing a thorough overhauling, one of them being a large tug from Galveston, which, besides having her woodwork renewed, will have a new and powerful set of boilers put into her.

It is the only railroad entering New Orleans that maintains its principal offices and shops within the city limits, where all the railroad repairs are made. In addition to this, all the repairs of the great fleet of steamships are made in Algiers, and every dollar expended for this purpose is put in circulation in this city and not in New York, the Northern end of the line. This enables a very large number of men to find daily employment year after year at good wages.

These steamships, together with the 2500 miles of railroad from Algiers to San Francisco, form the greatest through line for the transportation of freight from New York and all Atlantic seaboard points to San Francisco and beyond that exists to-day. The proof of this assertion is the fact that from 80 to 85 per cent. of all the freight between the Atlantic seaboard and the Pacific coast is shipped over it in the face of the competition of the several lines from New York to San Francisco. This large percentage has been maintained for years against the most active competition. The reason for it is that the time was made by the Southern Pacific route in several days faster time than that made by any other route.

The steamships reach New Orleans almost at a stated hour, indeed with nearly the regularity of a railroad train. In twelve hours the entire cargo is loaded in cars, and as fast as a trainload is ready an engine is coupled on and the train speeds on its way towards the Golden Gate, stopping only at terminals to change engines. The entire through line being under the same control, a decree of discipline and efficiency is attained that would not be possible under other circumstances, and this enables the Southern Pacific to make much better time than any of its Northern competitors, to maintain a great through line, landing traffic with regularity and dispatch and to distance its rivals by several days in time between New York and San Francisco.

Altogether, around the shops and wharf, there are employed during the busy season fully 3500 men, most of whom are residents of Algiers, and many have been in the employ of the company for many years. With such an institution in their midst, and giving the majority of her population bread and butter, is it any wonder that the people of Algiers appreciate the Southern Pacific Road?

——— ———

JOHN A. WOOD.

Wood, Schneidau AND Company, Coal Merchants,

WHOLESALE AND RETAIL.

Steamboat, Steamship, Plantations, Rice Mills, Cotton Presses, Foundries.

DEALERS AND FAMILIES SUPPLIES.

MAIN OFFICE:

43 Carondelet Street.

COAL YARD:

Foot of Race Street on Levee.

TELEPHONE 576.

New Orleans, La.

PAUL M. SCHNEIDAU.

The Grand Isle Road Orange Blossom Route.

Another railroad which has its terminus and the main portion of its plant in Algiers, is the New Orleans, Fort Jackson and Grand Isle Railroad, which has done much to add to the prosperity of this little burg. It was put in operation in 1890, and has never ceased, except when washouts caused a temporary suspension. Its depot is one of the first things to attract attention when you land in the town, and before the recent caving in of the river bank, which carried into the river more than three-quarters of the structure. It was an imposing looking building, and even now it is a credit to the place. Going up the cinder walk for a distance of 50 feet, there stretches out a well-kept garden which is quite a relief to the eye. The property of the company extends for several squares along the river front, but owing to the continued encroachments of the Father of Waters, great expense is incurred in trying to prevent further sloughing off into the river.

Further up the river, above the depot, is the roundhouse and machine shops, a neat little structure, amply large to suit the needs of the road. Altogether the road employs about 150 men, who are all residents of Algiers. The road is not in a completed state by any means, as it has two objective points one is Grand Isle, which its name implies, and the other is the old quarantine and Fort Jackson, down on the right bank of the Mississippi. There has not been any disposition to push the work of construction, owing to the depression in the money markets for the past year or two, but there is no telling how soon the work will be undertaken and pushed to completion. So far there has been about $750,000 of capital invested in the road, and it might be well to mention that every nickel of the capital stock is owned in the State of Louisiana.

There is one particularly noticeable feature of this road, and that is that its equipment is all of the very best and most modern that there is in the city of New Orleans. The coaches are all equipped with improved lavratories and have cane seats, which tend greatly to the comfort of the traveler. The track is standard guage, 60-pound steel rails, and as smooth as a floor.

The road is paying particular attention to the development of the truck farms on the lower coast, as these products are from two to four weeks earlier than on the other roads which transport them to the northern markets, which means a great deal.

A double daily train service is furnished the traveling public who have occasion to go down the coast at the present season of the year, while in the winter time four trains are sent out each day. Mr. J. S. Landry is the superintendent and has earned the esteem of all the employes.

The Dry Docks.

Almost as long as Algiers has been in existence, or, rather, ever since the shipping of the city of New Orleans has attained any proportions, Algiers has been the place where vessels were wont to go for docking and repairs, and each year the business has grown in proportion to the increase in the shipping of this port.

The first dry dock was constructed in 1837 at Paducah, Ky., and brought to Algiers the same year. A company was created by an act of the State Legislature

under the name of the New Orleans Floating Dry Dock Company, who became owners and managers thereof. The capital stock was $200,000. Captain L. Ma t thewes was president; G. E. Richardson, secretary and Gregory Burns, superintendent.

The second dock was built in Cairo, Ill., in 1840. It was bought by Captain James Stockton for account of himself and John Hughes. They subsequently transferred it to Bailey & Hughes. It proved a failure, and they destroyed it.

The third dock was brought from Pearlington, Miss., in 1843 by Captain Bailey and Peter Marcy, and was sunk shortly after. It was on the same principle as the Ocean Dock, with gates at the ends.

The Louisiana Dock was the fourth put into commission, and was built by the Louisiana Dock Company—J. P. Whitney, president; John Hughes, Francois Vallette and Mark Thomas, managers. It was a balance dock, closed at one end, and t the other there was a gate which was closed when raising craft.

The fifth was built in 1848 by Captain Bailey and Peter Marcy.

The next year the Pelican Dock was built, and it was the largest ever erected in Algiers. It was a sectional dock and had the capacity to lift a vessel 400 feet long. In 1857 it docked the steamer Eclipse, which was the largest, finest and heaviest steamboat that, either before or since the war, has floated in the Mississippi river. The dock was built by Charles Robinson, Mackie & Hyde, and was in service a long time before meeting with the usual fate.

In 1854 the seventh dock was built by the Crescent Docking Company, George W. Hynson, president, and Thos. Hasam and James Anderson, managers. It was called the Crescent. These parties subsequently controlled the Pelican Dock.

The eighth dock built was the Louisiana No. 3, by John Hughes and Francois Vallette. It was 265 feet long and 85 feet wide, and was built in 1855.

This year also saw the building of the ninth dock by Hyde & Mackie, which was a large section dock.

The tenth was built the following year by Mooney & Gerard. In 1856 the Fourth Louisiana dock was built by Hughes & Vallette, the Louisiana No. 3 having met with disaster. This one was 280 feet long by 89 feet wide, with a lifting power of 3500 tons.

The fourth Louisiana dock was built in 1860, in Pearlington, by Captain James Martin, and was named the Atlantic.

The thirteenth dock was built from the hull of the steamboat Illinois, by Tilton & Kalk, in 1863 or 1865.

The Southern dock was built in the west and went to work in 1864, under the management of D. O'Connor.

The Vallette dock was the fifteenth dock built in Algiers, and was put in operation in 1866, owned and built by the Vallette Dry Dock Company and was sunk several years ago. It was built across the lake in 1865 and completed in 1866.

The sixteenth dock was the Ocean, built in 1866, first owned by Mackie, Follette & Field, then by A. & O. I. McLellan and now by the McLellan Dock Company. It was towed down from Cairo in 1865, as an old barge, carrying 5000 bales of hay.

The seventeenth dock was also started in 1866, but was not put in operation until 1867. It was bought from the original owners by J. W. Black, who sold it to Major Robertson in 1888. It is the Marine dry dock.

The eighteenth dock was the Good Intent, which started to work in 18 -, and

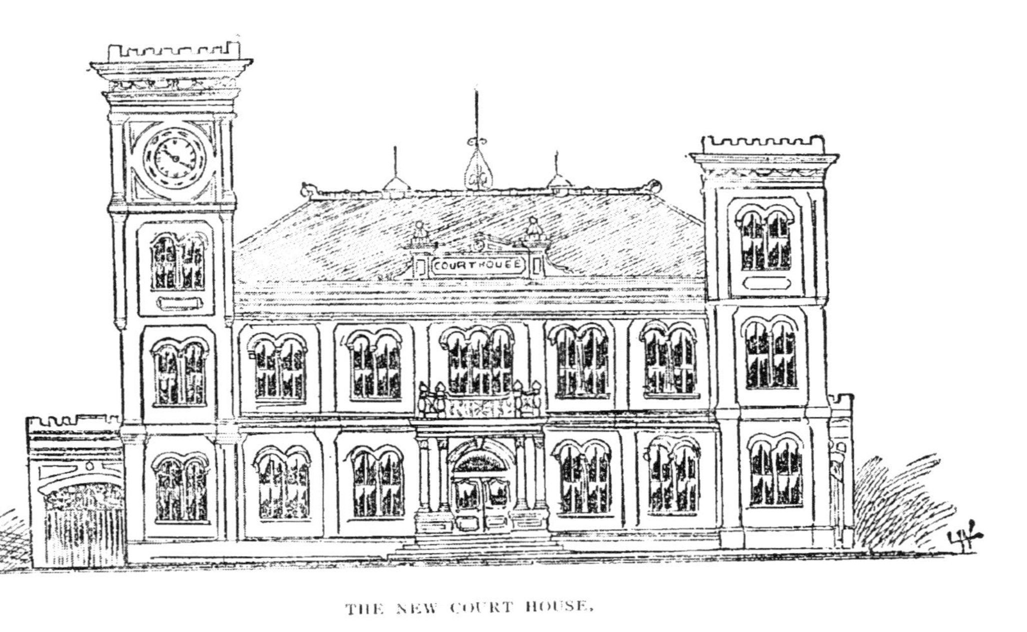

THE NEW COURT HOUSE.

is owned by the Red River Line.

The nineteenth was the Louisiana dry dock, and owned by McLellan, Brady & Cothell. It was lost in 1881.

John F. Follette and Captain O. P. Vallette built a large dock in Algiers in 1856 for use in the port of Havana, Cuba, where it was towed safely after completion. It was 300 feet long, 90 feet wide, with a lifting capacity of 5000 tons and sheathed with a very heavy coating of metal. It is in existence yet.

With this cursory glance into the past history of the docks of Algiers, a more extended look into the present state of that industry is in order. The first dock which attracts your attention as you go down the river is the Good Intent, owned by the Good Intent Dry Dock Company, of which Captain Charles P. Truslow is president and general manager. It is not of as imposing proportions as the other docks of Algiers, but it does its share of the business and employs upward of a score of men. The boats of the Red River Line are all docked here, as well as tugs and all classes of small boats.

The next is the Marine dock. It is the largest one in this section of the country at present, but its maximum capacity is only 1500 tons. The dock is 220 feet over all, but has docked the Clearwater, which is 250 feet long, the largest vessel which has ever been in it.

There are two engines, one on either side which can pump the largest vessels dry in less than two hours. The dock is what is known as a box, which, when ready to take on a ship, is filled with water and sunk, by means of opening valves. Then the vessel glides into the dock and when in position, the sliding blocks are pulled together, the shores let down, and then the pumps set to work to empty the water out of the dock. As it gradually rises out of the water, the shores and block are pulled taut, and by the time the ship is half out of the water she is as firmly fixed as if she were on the ways.

This company employs from 30 to 90 men as the occasion demands.

The Ocean dry dock is owned by the McLellan Dock Company, and is about three squares further down the river. It is very similar to the dock described above, is 204 feet long and 50 odd feet wide on the floor. It has been in operation since it was transformed from a large boat to a dock in 1865. The maximum capacity is about 1000 tons, and employs an average of 30 or 40 men the year round. Among the regular vessels taken care of here are those of the Interstate Transportation Company. It came into the possession of the present owners about eighteen years ago. The first boat ever docked by it was the blockade runner Lillian, near the close of the war. She overhung the dock and undocked herself during the night.

Away up the river, on the other side of the ferry landing, is the little dock of Wood, Schneidau & Co., where their tugs and others which may so desire, undergo the necessary repairs. This dock is worked by hand

The docking business of Algiers is a flourishing industry and gives employment to upwards of 200 or more men, which, considering the size of the town, is a most important feature of its industrial welfare.

Ship Building.

The ship-building industry of Algiers is one whose past is more glorious than its present, though its future gives promise of greater development than it has ever attained. Algiers is famous for its shipyards, but to walk along the levee a stranger would never suspect it. Many large boats were built over here. The latest being the Enterprise, in 1880, by the Southern Pacific Company. She was a monster transfer boat, and was built from the hull up, on the river bank near the great wharf. The same company also built the tug El Mozo two or three years ago. She was designed and constructed under the supervision of Captain Morse.

Richard Cogan's shipyard is situated at No. 1 Patterson street, on the river front. It was formerly known as Mahoney's shipyard, but was bought out by the present owner's father some time ago, and who had been in business for thirty years or more. It is within a stone's throw of the ferry landing, and, unless you went around by the front way and peered within, you would never suspect that it was a shipyard. There you see a barn-like structure about 75 feet long and 40 feet wide, with an open space to the river. In here Mr. Cogan, with his half dozen assistants, builds all kinds of small craft from 50-foot pleasure boats to 10-foot skiffs. A good portion of his business is building lighters for the Central American trade.

Other Industries.

The Algiers Waterworks and Electric Light Company is a comparatively new institution in Algiers, and has flourished from its incipiency. It was put in operation in 1892, and is located on the square bounded by Elmira, Thayer, Pelican and Pacific avenues. It supplies nearly all the ice used in Algiers and electric lights for commercial purposes, also water for all. The capital invested is somewhere in the neighborhood of $85,000, and from twelve to fifteen men are given continuous employment. In ice-making the anhydrous ammonia absorption process is in use, in which the gas is set free from its water solution by heat, is condensed, expanded and then reabsorbed by the water. There are two 10-ton machines, invented by Thoens & Gerdes, of New Orleans, and the plant in its entirety is of home production, and exceeds its guaranteed output by 25 per cent. Each machine consists of a retort, exchanger, absorber, condenser, cooler, ammonia pump, rectifier and freezing tank. There are 300 molds, each holding 105 pounds of ice. Six to seven pounds of ice are made to every pound of coal used, and the molds use 250 gallons of cooling water per minute. The water is from an artesian well 840 feet deep, is condensed and rendered tasteless and odorless. The main pump has a capacity of 400 gallons per minute. An 85-horse power boiler supplies the steam. There is a 4600 electric light dynamo, which completes the plant. Everything is as neat and clean as a pin, and th plant is modernly fitted up throughout. Mr. Foster Olroyd is the superintendent.

The Algiers saw mill is the only one in the place, and has been established for about fifteen years. It is located on the river front, about midway between two large docks, and gives steady employment to about thirty men the year round. It saws up about 1,500,000 feet of timber a year, besides the supplies received by rail. It occupies about 300 feet of the front and runs back some distance. The special features of the business is supplying the steamship trade with spars, masts, derricks, booms and general boat timbers. It is a distinct business, and this mill has a monopoly of it in New Orleans. The local trade is supplied with house lumber of all kinds as well. The proprietors are Messrs. Peter S Lawton and Albert E. Hotard.

A mile up the river is the Security Brewing Company's plant, a modern brick structure, fully equipped, and having a capacity of 40,000 barrels a year. The building was erected in 1891 and the brewery put into operation, but it met with financial reverses and was placed in the hands of a receiver, who on July 21 last turned it over to the new owners, some parties from St. Louis, who intend to make many improvements and supply the entire trade of Algiers in a short time. They claim to supply the bulk of it now, and are even reaching after C ty trade, having a depot in New Orleans. About forty-five men are regularly employed. The capital stock of the reorganized Company is $150,000. Superintendent Henry Reninger is the "brau meister," and his brew of the amber-tinted nectar is quite delicious.

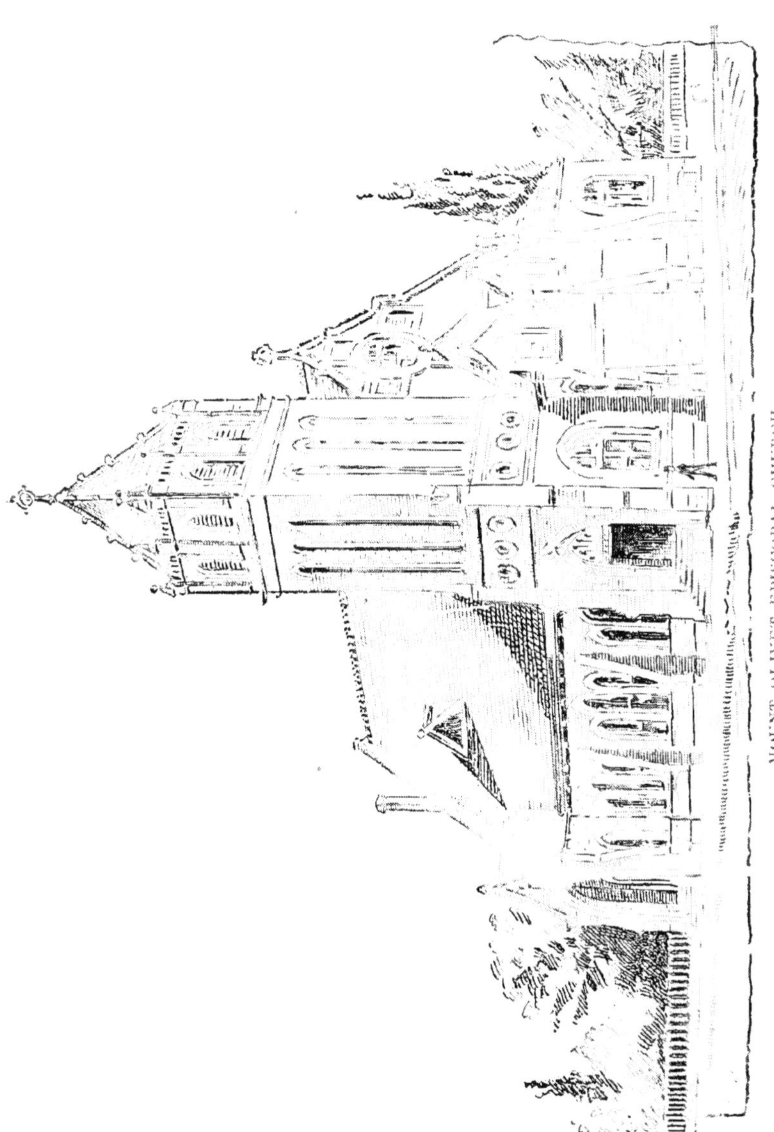

MOUNT OLIVET EPISCOPAL CHURCH.

There is a street car line in Algiers running from the ferry landing to Gretna, which is owned by Captain Pickles, and it is a great convenience to the residents of the town as well as those residing above. The ferry service cannot be omitted, for it is one of the greatest necessities of Algiers; and keep in close touch with New Orleans. Captain Pickles seems to have filled the wants of the people in that regard. He has given us the best ferry system we ever had since the first steam ferry in 1828. Capt. Alex. Halliday, his superintendent, always courteous and obliging. Is constantly on the alert, and is truly the right man in the right place.

A New Station for the Southern Pacific was Opened November 27th, 1895.

The beautiful station was opened to the use of the public that morning, when train No. 21 west-bound came across the river on the steam transfer Endeavor. Not one hitch occurred and the entire apparatus worked admirably. When the signal was given that the transfer was ready to deliver its load of cars to the station proper, the engine gave a loud blast of its whistle and then the first passenger train ever under the roof of the new station climbed up the bridge. Hundreds of people were standing about to see it enter the station, and it was plain that they looked upon the event with delight. Soon afterwards the train was ready to proceed westward.

Not long after the outgoing train had left, the echo of an engine whistle was heard some distance out the road, and in a few minutes the local passenger train from Lafayette, No. 54, due at 10:48 a. m., rounded into the station "on the dot." The passengers aboard knew that something unusual had occurred, else they would have been pulled into the old station. Hence, nearly every passenger on the train got off and took a glance at the new station, all pronouncing it an immense improvement over the old order of things, with the facilities for rapid transit, for which the Southern Pacific is noted. No. 51 was soon ready to cross the river to New Orleans station. The whistle was blown, the passengers boarded the coaches and then the train glided down the incline on to the transfer boat, which drew back out of the ways and was shortly afterward landed on the east bank of the river. There were no ceremonies accompanying the opening of the public.

The new station is a model one, perhaps the handsomest in any Southern city. It is a frame structure with corrugated roofs. The entire inside is of oak, varnished, while the outer walls are painted tastefully. The station occupies the space between Elmira and Vallette streets, on the levee, and is about 300 feet long and 50 feet in height. The width is 75 feet. Running through the station there are four tracks with switches leading to the incline, This is worked automatically by hydraulic pressure, and when the river is low the incline lowers. When there is a rise in the river the incline raises. Between the tracks is laid concrete gravel, and the platforms are on either side of them. Leading to the incline is the ticket office and baggage-room. Altogether it is a modern and complete railroad station, and surpasses anything yet built of its kind in this City.

Eureka Homestead Society,

323 BARONNE STREET, Next to Corner Union Street,

ORGANIZED, 2ND DECEMBER, 1884.

$187,500 LOANED ON HOMES IN ALGIERS.

1189 Shares, $594,500 Held in Algiers.

Earnings from
8 per cent. to
28 per cent.
per annum!
$1,450,000
Capital Stock
Subscribed
For . . . .

P. J. MAGUIRE,
President, Eureka Homestead Society.

TWO SERIES MATURED AND PAID OFF.

SERIES "A" Earned a profit of $221.69 per Share of $500, or $278.31 paid in Monthly, an average Profit of nearly 17 per cent. per annum.

SERIERS "B" Earned a prcfit of $205.50 per Share of $500, or $294.50 paid in monthly; an average profit of nearly 14½ per cent. per annum.

$2.50 Per Share of $500 per Month, is all you pay. $1000 costs $5.00 per month only until you borrow. Then $1000 costs you but $10 per month.

$458,000.00 IN REAL ESTATE GIVES ABSOLUTE SECURITY.

OFFICERS:

P. J. MAGUIRE, President; HUGH McMANUS, Vice President;
JAS. T. RODD, Treasurer; BERNARD McCLOSKEY, Atty;
E. J. BARNETT, Notary; W. H. PREIS, Secretary.

DIRECTORS—Jas. A. Acomb, F. C. Brinkman, D. Danziger, Chas. W. Drown, Horace Fletcher, Thornwell Fay, Wm. A. Gordon, Isidore Heckinger, J. E. Jackson, J. J. Kuhner, J. M. Leonhard, P. J. Maguire, Francis Martin, Jno. T. Michel, Robt. G. Memory, Mat. A. Morse, Hugh McManus, Jno. P. Nolan, R. L. Preis, Jas. T. Rodd, W. L. Saxon, E. M. Underhill, J. B. Vinet, H. M. Verlander, Robt. W. Wilson.

323 BARONNE ST., Next to Corner Union St.

COMMITTEES:

REAL ESTATE—General Jno. B. Vinet, Jas. T. Rodd, Robt. G. Memory.
FINANCES—Walter L. Saxton, Colonel E. M. Underhill, Isidore Heckinger.
SPECIAL COMMITTE ON SOCIETY'S REAL ESTATE—Hugh McManus.
INSPECTOR—Robt. G. Memory.

Mr. C. M. Jennings, of the Algiers Democrat, had the distinction of purchasing the first ticket in the new station that morning. He purchased a round-trip ticket to Gretna Green and return, and will keep the little piece of pasteboard in commemoration of the fact.

The Old Duverje Mansion.

The Algiers Court House, formerly so familiar to the residents of the Fifth District, was among the oldest bui dings in this part of the State and was an excellent idea of what a family mansion was in the early part of the present century.

The old Court House has been known as the Duverje house as far back as 1812, and was a massive structure, built of brick, with solid masonry laid in adamantine cement. The gigantic pillars around the house upholding the galleries and roof, presented a firm front to the inroads of time. From one of the galleries of the mansion an excellent view of the river was obtained, and the old residents well wonder over the changes that have taken place in Algiers since 1812. At that time Algiers was not dreamed of. Plantations and orange groves made up the surrounding country.

The Court House was built with the strength of a fortress, and when Mr. Duverje was engaged in its construction his friends remonstrated with him, suggesting that the site selected was a bad one, as it would be gradully washed away by the river. Not only has this failed to occur, but the house was so substantially built that it bid fair to last many a long year, when it was destroyed by fire, Oct. 20, 1895. The shingles on the roof remained intact for sixty years, and when it was decided to put a new roof on, the new roof was found to be but little better than the old one. The bricks were made in the brick yards then situated on the river bank in the front of the estate. Mr. Barthelemy Duverje, who was a good mechanic, personally superintended the erection of the building.

After the death of Mrs. Widow Duverje, in 1830, the estate was divided among the heirs and Mrs. Evelina Duverje-Olivier, her daughter, received the fine old mansion, together with her share of the land adjoining.

Mr. Duverje purchased the plantation site on which the building stands from Martial Le Bœuf, Aug. 9, 1805. The latter's title is traced to Louis Borepo, who acquired Feb. 3, 1770, by grant from Don Alexander O'Reilly, Governor of the province of Louisiana, who then represented the crown of Castile under Charles III. Some eighty years ago the late J. B. Olivier led Alix. Duverje to the handsome octagon, corniced room in the center of the building, where they were joined together in matrimony in the presence of many of the old regime. The room was last occupied as a City Court.

A century has gone by since the cabildo of O'Reilly's regime had alienated the land. It is difficult to realize all that transpired on the spot. From the galleries of the house was heard the cannonding on the field of Chalmette on the 8th of January, 1815, In the orange groves adjoining rested many a merry group from Tchou-Tchouma, "the home of the sun." To the same spot came John McDonogh on many an occasion to while away an evening hour. Years passed on. From the upper windows anxious faces gaze forth at the Smoky City; around the bend steams slowly by Farragut and the Federal fleet.

Its a Short Cut

That's all it is—a quick and convenient way to gain possession of what home lacks.

You want to make your house cosy and comfortable.

Here and there a change is needed to brighten up the appearances of your apartments.

The **Bedroom** needs new Matting, Shades or Lace Curtains, a few pretty Rugs, one or two Comfortable Rockers and a pretty Mantel Mirror would add materially to the attractiveness of the **Parlor**—or perhaps you need a Stove for the **Kitchen.**

We have an immense line of **House Furnishing Goods** in stock; your choice of which we offer you for cash or on a fair and equitable credit system.

T. DUMAS CO., LTD.,

The Home Furnishers,

922 AND 924 CANAL STREET.

FRED. W. ABBOT.

Again, in the month of April, 1865, another scene is witnessed. The Webb goes swiftly down stream, displaying the Confederate flag for the last time, and perished a few miles below the city. The occupant of the house then was Father George Lamey, a cure, who had served under Napoleon in Africa.

At a meeting of the Police Jury of Algiers, held Jan. 5, 1869, the following resolution offered by the writer, then president of said body, was adopted:

"Whereas, the buildings situated on Delaronde street, at present occupied by the parish authorities for public business, are totally unfit for said purposes and for years past a disgrace to the parish.

"Resolved, That the improvement committee are hereby empowered to take possession of the Duverje mansion, belonging to the parish, on Villere street, to make all requisite repairs, and to obtain such furniture as may be deemed requisite."

The local paper of Algiers, March, 1869, tells the story thus: "The repairs and improvements made upon the Duverje mansion are now completed, and the authorities, having abandoned the old courthouse on Delaronde street, will soon take possession of the former. Henceforth, the edifice will be alive with all 'pomp and circumstance' attendant upon the administrators of public affairs. For the jury will have its sitting there, the justice will hold court there, the collector his taxes. 'The man with a grievance' will find his way there to indulge in the luxury of the law; the time-honored tribe of grumblers, whose generations, reaching far beyond the period when the Israelites growled at Moses, go back to the time when Cain grew wroth at the doings of Abel, will make that the focus of all discontent. Meanwhile, the abandoned old court building stands like 'some banquet hall deserted,' only, perhaps, a little more 'seedy.' Some gem of song inculcates the prudence of being 'off with the old love before being on with the new.' In deference to this incalculation, it may be well to take leave of the forlorn old quintessence of shabbiness before paying court to its handsome successor."

The old mansion became the seat of justice of the right bank on March 13, 1869. Many visitors were present on the occasion.

The manner in which the improvements had been completed reflected credit both on the committee, who devised the plans, and the artisans who executed them. All the work was done by Algiers mechanics.

The parish of Orleans, right bank, was annexed to the city on March 14, 1870, and designated as the Fifth District. The courthouse was one of the assets. It was, up to the great fire, in excellent condition, well worthy of a visit, and gave one an idea of how Creole homes were constructed during le vieux regime.

Olden Times. McDonogh's Letter.

The most thoroughly equipped and disciplined body of citizen solidierly that Louisiana ever possessed in ante bellum times was, without contest, the organization popularly known as the Legion. Its origin dates from the period of our territorial government At that time several companies, composed of Creoles and of Frenchmen, who had seen active service in Europe, were formed. They constituted the nuecles, around which gathered in subsequent years, other similar organizations, so that, when in 1814, the British invaded our soil, a body of troops known as the Battalion of Orleans Volunteers, were ready to take the field without delay.

HAMILTON R. GAMBLE.

Their services and poweress are now a part of our country's history. In the course of time this small crops increased in strength and stability with such rapidity that it was incorporated into a legion commanded by Generals of repute, such as Cuvellier, De Buys, Lewis and Augustin. This is a brief outline of its existence. Nearly every nationality was represented in this organization. The Germans had their Yaegers, the Spaniards, their Cazadores, the French their Voltigeurs, Cuirassiers and Lancers, the Americans their Washington Guards and Louisiana Grays, the Creoles their Grenadiers, their Sappers and Miners, each appareled in appropriate and gaudy uniforms. There was even a mounted corps of Mamelukes. The Orleans Battalion of Artillery, under the direction of the noted Dominique You and Major Gally, was complete in every detail, and ever ready for active service.

By special act of the Legislature the Legion was required to assist the Mayor in all cases of tumult when the police found themselves unable to preserve the public peace, and in April, 1830, the City voted it a yearly allowance of $2000 in compensation for the service.

About that time the Louisiana Legion turned out in a body to go through the evolutions of a "petite guerre" or sham battle in Marigny's field, jointly with the uniformed companies of the First Brigade, which had been invited for the occasion. About 520 men of the Fourth Regiment of the United States regulars, stationed in the City under Major's Twiggs, appeared and formed a reserve corps, in the rear of three columns of attack, headed by Lieut. Col. Cuvellier and directed against a point which was defended by 200 infantry and two field pieces, under the command of Major Daunoy. The onset being irresistible, a pontoon bridge was thrown by the latter over the Marigny's canal. A retreat was ordered. This operation enabled him to take a new position on the opposite bank, and to resist with advantage a body of troops much stronger than his own, supported by two field pieces and two troops of cavalry under Capts, Vignie and Ed. Ducros. The mimic conflict was admirably planned and conducted, and after the firing had ceased, a copious breakfast champetre, offered to the general staff, the United States troops and the uniformed companies of the brigade, terminated a military feast, which was marred by no accident and attended throughout by the most hearty good nature and cordiality. In addition to two cavalry companies from Jefferson, there were two companies from St. Bernard, the Louisiana Guards, the Lafayette Rifleman and the Cadets, who, with the United States troops and the Legion, formed a total of nearly 1500 men, of all arms, when they re-entered the City.

The object of the Legion was to encourage military ardor and discipline. Every holiday, or State occasion, was taken advantage of to exhibit this spirit. Thus on St. Barbe's Day, the patroness of artilleries, the Orleans Battalion, were wont to turn out in splendid array, with a bouquet of flowers inserted in their "mousquetons," and proceed to the Cathedral to hear mass and take up a subscription for the orphans' asylums. This yearly practice was religiously observed every December. Their flags and banners were usually blessed by the Bishop in the progress of some ceremony. Every Sunday witnessed some marked display or procession, whether the soldiers were to drill on the Place d'Armes, or on their way to some rural retreat. In connection with these excursions to the country, the following "card," from the eccentric philanthropist, John McDonogh, finds an

STEAMER THOS. PICKLES

appropriate place here, as characteristic of the man and of the times :

TO THE PUBLIC.

"My name, having appeared in the Bee of Monday, the 12th instant, (April, 1841,) in a piece headed 'Arvis,' and signed 'Un Garde d'Orleans,' in relation to a very trifling occurence, I should have let pass unheeded and without notice, but my friends thinking otherwise, I am induced to give, in a few words, the facts as they took place.

"On Sunday morning last, the 11th instant, between the hours of 9 and 10 o'clock, two gentlemen in military costume came into my house, opposite the City, and requested me to permit their military company to go into my garden and pavilion, for the purpose of giving a 'breakfast.' I informed them politely that I could not; that, having refused a similar permission, at different times, for the last two years, to various military companies, I could not permit them to go in, as I would thereby lay myself liable to reproach from those I refused.

"This reply and refusal did not satisfy the gentlemen, who insisted strenously on the use of my private property, and it was in vain that I observed to them repeatedly that they had my answer. They were not to be refused. At length one of them insinuated in his language that they were willing to pay for the privilege, when I instantly observed to them: 'Very well, gentlemen, it shall be so. I ask you nothing, not a cent, for myself. Take the pen and paper (pointing to it, as it lay on my table) and draw a note, payable to the order of the Orphan Asylum Society, for the sum of $250, which is about $4 a head for each of your company, and you shall go in and enjoy its pleasures; and to-morrow morning I will put a notice in the Gazette, informing the military companies of the City in general that they will be permitted to use may garden and pavilion whenever they think proper on the same conditions.' But the charity of the gentlemen, it appeared, did not extend quite so far, as they merely observed that they could not accede to my proposition, and immediately withdrew.

"The foregoing is, word for word, what took place between us: The 'Orleans Guard' in said piece invites particularly all such persons as desire to serve the Patrie, to address themselves immediately to me. For this high mark of regard and distinction, I thank the Guard, and will only observe (though I never speak of myself, except when I am forced by circumstances), that whenever they (the Orleans Guards) shall have rendered such services to the Patrie as the writer of this (though a very humble individual), has had the good fortune to render it, that the gates of his garden and his house shall be at all times flung open night or day) whenever they (the Guards) approach them, to do them honor. To conclude, I will now state to the public what I did not state or say (from motives of delicacy, to those gentlemen in the interview above alluded to. I have been for fifteen years at great expense in establishing this garden, and formerly, and until the last two years, was in the habit of permitting the militia companies of the city to enter it, exercise on the pavilion and take their repast there. But I was forced about that time to a resolution never again to permit, so illy was I rewarded by some of those to whom I had granted the privilege, in having my trees, shrubbery, plants and flowers cut up, destroyed and even pulled up by the roots, in several instances and carried away.

"JOHN M'DONOGH.

FROM MEMORY BY
JOHN N RILEY. 29

—THE—

Algiers Waterworks and Electric Company,

Was organized on the 29th day of October, 1895, by Messrs. E. L. Bemiss, Charles Carroll, F. A. Daniels, W. P. Nicholls, W. T. Hardie, A. E. Hotard and their associates. The waterworks rights and franchises of the New Orleans Waterworks Company were then purchased for Algiers, thus giving the newly organized company the exclusive water privilege for that district during the next forty years. The company then decided upon the purchase of the plant of the Algiers Ice and Electric Company, which was for sale, as affording a suitable location for the waterworks plant and also giving an established business in the beginning. This done, the work of construction of the waterworks plant was then taken up. This was begun in December, 1895, and completed in April, 1896, the company opening its plant for the service of the public on May 1st, 1896.

The distribution system consists of nearly 12 miles of street mains, varying in size from 6 inches to 14 inches, and supplying water to 200 fire plugs for the use of the city for fire purposes.

In the pumping station, which is built of brick and steel, and is absolutely fireproof throughout, are located two duplex Worthington steam pumping engines, each having a normal capacity of 3,000,00 gallons of water per day.

Connected with the pumps and water mains is the standpipe, 120 feet high and 16 feet in diameter, which will keep a steady pressure of 60 pounds per square inch on the mains, and which will furnish sufficient pressure to extinguish any ordinary fire without the aid of steam engine.

The company also operates an Electric Light Plant, and furnishes electric light for private consumption in Algiers, having a capacity of about 2000 16 candle power incandescent lamps.

The Ice Manufacturing part of the works is equipped with two 10-ton ice machines of the absorption system, with a total capacity of 20 tons every 24 hours.

The whole plant is complete, and in every respect a model one for efficiency and economy in operation.

The officers of the company are as follows:

E. L. BEMISS, President; WM. T. HARDIE, Vice President;
LEIGH CARROLL, Secretary and Treasurer;
FOSTER OLROYD, Superintendent.

The Directors are:

WM. T. HARDIE, WM. P. NICHOLLS, E. L. SIMONDS,
F. A. DANIELS, A. E. HOTARD, J. B. CRAVEN,
CHARLES CARROLL, E. L. BEMISS,
AND THE MAYOR OF THE CITY OF NEW ORLEANS, Ex-Officio.

Lost McAllister.

The advent of the new year brings many happy events of the past to recollection; but to others in our midst, it has its sorrows. From 1870 to 1877 Captain Chas. W. Howell was major of engineers in this department in the government service, having under his supervision, among other duties, that of removing the obstructions at the Passes, in order to keep the channel clear prior to the construction of the Jetties, at the mouth of the river.

Two vessels, the Essayon and McAlister, powerful steam dredges, were constructed under his supervision especially for that object. It was deemed advisable to send one of the boats to Sabine Pass to accomplish their object.

The McAllister was brought up to Algiers and received a thorough repairing at the Ocean Dry Dock, Olivier street, before proceeding on the journey. The vessel left here with her crew on the 31st of December, 1877. Capt. Warren was master, and LeRoy Swift, his assistant, Joseph Heap, engineer and William Beaver as captain's clerk, together with others from this town in different capacities. The vessel crossed the bar and proceeded upon her voyage January 1, 1878 From that date naught has been heard of the ship or crew. All must have perished as no vestige of the wreck was ever recovered or a body seen.

There was much suffering amongst the families in consequence, but active work was soon taken in their behalf. A relief committee was appointed, James H. Finegan, as chairman and Messrs. Manuel Abascal, Joseph Lyons. William Sarazin, Joseph Hughes and others on the executive committee, who soon did noble work for unfortunates whose breadwinners had been so ruthlessly torn from them. E. John Ellis and R. L. Gibson were in the House of Representatives as members from Louisiana and B. F. Jonas the Senator. A bill for the relief of the families was introduced in Congress. The committee here determined the advisability of having some one upon the spot to make known the distress and the urgent necessity of prompt action and relief. Judge Seymour was the gentleman selected, who at once proceeded to Washington and gave full information, calling also upon President Hayes who became deeply interested and gave the measure his hearty approval. In a few days the bill became a law and one year's salary was appropriated to each family whose support had perished and paid in due time by a special officer sent on to New Orleans for that purpose.

A board of inquiry was subsequently appointed to ascertain the sea worthiness of the vessel prior to her departure. Considerable testimony was taken, but the prevailing opinion was that the ship was too top heavy and filled with cumbersome machinery, which became unmanageable, that the ship eventually went over in the trough of the seas, and all went to the bottom of the gulf.

A Historical Home—Written in 1889.

About one mile below Algiers, facing the river, is the hamlet of Tunisburg, which has a frontage of two blocks on the public road and extending in depth to the woods. On either side of the village may be seen the beautiful residences of the Trepagniers, Webert, Lawton, and Willet, delightfully situated amid orange and peach orchards, flowers and shrubbery. Far out the trees are festooned with

MARINE DRY DOCK.

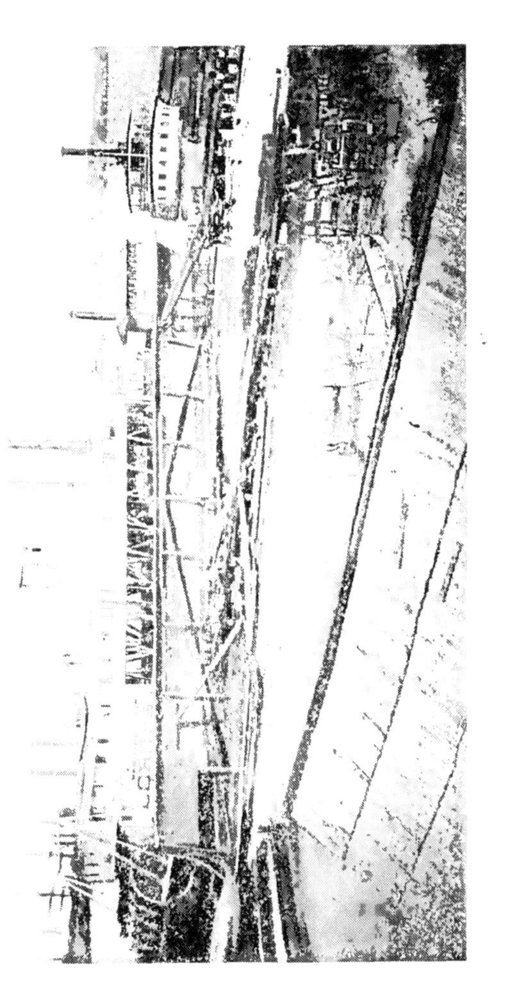

great draperies of Spanish moss, wreathing and drooping from limb to limb; the forests are densely filled with rank vegetable growth of various kinds, notably the palmetto bush, spreading out like a fan, which forms barriers against explorers, only to be broken down by patient labor with the axe. Two blocks back from the river stands the ruins of an old fashioned mansion surrounded by a grove of cedar trees, a mansion wherein W. B. Howell, father-in-law of Jefferson Davis, resided with his family for awhile. Mr. Howell being at the time Naval Officer of the Customs at the Port of New Orleans. In this residence was passed many a day of Varina Banks Howell, widow of the chieftain, and Beckett Howell, subsequently of the "Sumpter," and the brother who perished so nobly, in command of his ship on the Pacific since the termination of the civil war.

Some of our old citizens who still reside in the LOCALE in question, remember the happy group who were wont to assemble upon a pleasant summer eve at decline of sun upon the levee where one could hear the vesper bells from the Ursuline convent just opposite, and see the falling rays upon the monument at the field of Chalmette while at their feet

"The Father of Waters rolling,
 On in its pomp and pride,
Caressing the dormant galleys,
 Nested closely side by side,
And proudly sweeping by,
 Where at the close of day,
It circles in its course,
Where the Crescent City lay."

Of that group, one is now a widow, her cup of grief has surely overflown. Another was conveyed to his resting place in the beautiful Metairie, followed by thousands of sympathizers. There he slept for a while—

"Beneath one in granite,
 By the hand of genius made,
Once again to rise before us,
 Waiting for his "Old Brigade;"
Chieftain—Hero—Christain—Soldier,
 King of men, and man of God,
Crytalized about his foot steps,
 Greatness the ground he trod."

Mr. Davis bought the old home from his relative on the 3rd of January, 1853, and it continued to be his property, which he occasionally visited from Mississippi until it was seized by the United States authorities and sold under the confiscation act, by Cuthbert Bullitt, then United States Marshal, in May, 1865. It was bought by Joseph Cazaubon, of Tunisburg, for a nominal sum. This sale only annulled the life interest of Jefferson Davis in the property, but did not touch his heirs. In the month of September, 1872, Jefferson Davis and Varina Howell, his wife, for due consideration, renounced to Mr. Cazaubon all future claim to the property for themselves and heirs.

The old home stands, but its old owner now rests "Where the first rays of the morning's sunlight and the last gleam of the evening will linger around the silent, solitary sentinel, and in the still, quiet watches of the night, when the pale moonbeams fall upon the dreamless sleepers; there the spirit of the great Stonewall

JOHN M'DONOGH

Abstracts From Memoranda Addressed by John McDonogh to the Executors of His Estate.

"The Plan which my mind formed (influenced, I trust by the Divine Spirit) and has pursued, for nearly Forty Years, to accumulate and get together a large Estate, in lands, lots of ground, in and near the City, Houses, etc., for the Education of the Poor, will in time, I doubt not, yield a revenue sufficient to educate all the Poor of the two States, of Louisiana and Maryland, and perhaps the poor of many other States in our Happy Union. To effect and secure that, I have laid its Foundations deep and broad, in and all around the City of New Orleans in every direction, so that for centuries to come (of managed in wisdom) its Revenue must and will go on increasing in amount with the growth and entension of the City (which is destined to be one of the greatest in extent and Population the world has ever seen) until its Rents shall amount to some millions of dollars annually. If therefore those who will come after me, and will have the management of this store (which I have strove to amass and pile up) will labor to increase and render it productive with the same fidelity which I have husbanded it, and striven to make it a great one, then indeed, it will become in time a huge mountain of wealth, and will yield its increase to the Honor of God, and the benefit of Generations yet unborn, through all Ages of the World."

"In relation to man's happiness, constituted as he is, I have always been convinced that the intellectual cultivation of the Youth of our Country ALONE without religious cultivation cannot secure it, or give permanency to the Free Institutions of the Country, as they now exist. Education, separated from Religion, yields no security to morality and Freedom."

"I trust, I pray, that the mode I have adopted to effectuate it, will receive the Divine Blessing. I have, notwithstanding, much, very much, to complain of the World, rich as well as Poor. It has harassed me in a thousand different ways. Suits at law, of great injustice have been instituted and carried on against me, to deprive and take from me, property, honestly acquired, (for I have none, nor even would have any that was not acquired by honest industry and the sweat of my brow), and when obliged to seek justice through Courts of Law (after waiting years and years with those who were indebted to me, and refused payment) it has often and often been refused me. Many and many times have juries of my fellow men given me a stone when I asked them for bread."

"They said of me, he is rich, old, without wife or child, let us take from him then what he has. Infatuated men, they knew not that was an attempt to take from themselves, for I was laboring, and had labored all my life, not for myself, but for them and their children. Their attempts, however, made me not to swerve, either to the right hand or to the left (although to see, and to feel so sorely their injustice and ingratitude, made me often to lament the frailty, the perversity, and sinfulness of our fallen nature). I preserved an onward course, determined (as the Steward and Servant of my Master) to do them good, whether they would have it, or whether they would not have it. And I have so strove, so labored to the last; the result is in the hands of Him who fixes and determines all results; He will do therewith as seemeth good unto himself.

STATEMENT OF APPORTIONMENT OF THE REAL ESTATE OF JOHN McDONOGH

BETWEEN THE CITIES OF NEW ORLEANS AND BALTIMORE.

Location of property.	New Orleans.	Baltimore.
First District of New Orleans	$230,000 00	$230,000 00
Second " "	135,785 00	154,380 00
Third " "	88,400 00	81,200 00
	$454,845 00	$466,480 00
Parish of Orleans	17,000 00	6,825 00
Town McDonogh, Parish Orleans	20,100 00	
" " " Jefferson	11,200 00	32,801 00
Parish of Jefferson	34,685 00	30,015 00
" St. Bernard		2,020 00
" St. James	44,000 00	75,000 00
" Lafourche, interior	1,500 00	
" Plaquemines	56,020 00	
" East Baton Rouge	40,000 00	
" St. Tammany	200 00	
" Livingston	3,400 00	7,000 00
" Assumption	11,000 00	
" St. Landry	210 00	
" St. Charles	200 00	
" Iberville		81,500 00
	$704,440 00	$704,440 00
Total	$1,408,880 00	

McDonogh's Last Receipt.

CONTRIBUTED FOR THE STORY OF ALGIERS BY O. CHARLES OLIVIER, ESQ.

"Received of Mr. Wm. W. Filkins, Twenty-five Dollars, it being one month's rent, say from the 1st day of September last, until the 1st day of October, instant, of the lot of ground occupied by you, as per lease from me, situated on the corner of Magazine and Girod streets, in the suburbs St. Mary, 2d Municipality of New Orleans.

JOHN McDONOGH,

$25. NEW ORLEANS, October 1st, 1850."

loosened for awhile from the prison-house of the departed," will wander forth to guard his chief, and the noble band who lie slumbering there at rest.

HOW BEAUTIFUL,

how again appropiate occurs to memory the other sentiments, voiced by Fitz Hugh Lee, in the presence of Mr. Davis, on the same hallowed spot some eight years before.

"Now, when the wand of peace is waving wide through sea and land; now, when no war or battle sound is heard; now, when the idle shield and spear are high uphung, and the broken chariot stands, with the soldiers' blood, gallant survivors of a gallant band are grouped around a monument, which will stand in lofty and lasting attestation to commemorate their love, for the memory of the great Commander."

Yes, yon granite minstrel's voiceless stone,
    In deathless song shall tell,
When many a vanished year has flown,
    The story how he fell—
Nor wreck, nor change, nor winter's bright,
    Nor time's remorseless doom shall dim one ray,
Of Holy light that gilds his glorious tomb."

Mount Olivet Church.--Episcopal.

This handsome edifice of worship was erected in 1894-5. Much taste is displayed in its construction, which is of brick and of the Gothic order. The decoration are worthy of the sacredness of the place. The colored glass of the windows throws a beautiful mellowed light across the aisle, producing a chastened effect, suited to the solemnity of the place. Immediately above the altar is a memorial window, to the memory of the Rev. C. S. Hedges, a deceased pastor of the church, a respected man beloved by all, who died 2d April, 1892; design of which memorial is executed with the bold hand of a master. Take this altogether, it is one of the neatest houses of devotion in the town; and a pretty specimen of ecclesiastical architecture. The corner-stone was laid with much ceremony, May 3d, 1894; the old frame building church having been removed to the rear of the property, where it is now used as a school.

Service was first held in the new building November 25th, 1894. McDonald Bros., of Louisville, Ky., were the architects, J. F. Barnes the builder, and Felix J. Borne superintendent.

To the Reverend Arthur Howard Noll, twelfth rector of Mount Olivet, must be awarded all credit and praise for the indefatiguable energy, push and vim, displayed from beginning to end in the erection of the edifice; who was well encouraged throughout by the ladies of the congregation, the vestry and building committee, despite many obstacles to be overcome during the construction; not omitting the scores of kind friends of other denominations and members, who so cheerfully contributed as their means would permit for the object.

The property was purchased from J. B. Olivier, 3rd December, 1852, and consisted then of two vacant lots of ground, forming the corner of Olivier and Pelican avenue. Prior to that period services were held at intervals in the basement of the old Hughes Hotel, under the auspices of the Rev. Dr. Whithall, commencing in 1846.

M'DONOGH SCHOOL NO. 4.

A charter was granted to "Mount Olivet Church" by Joseph Walker, Governor of Louisiana, January 18th, 1853, which was certified to by Charles Gayarre, then Secretary of State, 21st January of that year, the charter issued under the general law regarding like corporations, enacted 30th April, 1847. The charter members designated were: James Duncan, Gordon C. Fory, Robert Roberts, Jacob Nelson, Thomas Hughes, Augustine Fory and Alexander Reid. In addition, James Cooke and A. G. Vandenberg were included as vestrymen.

The wooden church building, wherein religious services were conducted from 1853 to 1895, was twice badly damaged by fire, both occasioned by defective flues; the first time, during 1868, and again, January 8th, 1893. Active measures were at once taken and same rebuilt, which now occupies the rear portion of the lots facing on Pelican avenue, used first as a parish Episcopal school.

The charter of the church was lost with other papers during one of these fiery ordeals. This was a matter of considerable vexation; efforts were made to obtain a certified copy from the State Department at Baton Rouge, the result was futile, most of the State records were destroyed by fire while the Capitol Building was burning while occupied by Federal soldiers, in 1862.

Eventually the document was recovered in a most unexpected manner. The debris of one of the fires was carted away and thrown on the river bank in Algiers. Some one found it there on the shore of the great river, and placed same in possession of of Capt. Henry Willett, who was the medium of promptly restoring it to the vestry and wardens of the church.

Some objections having arisen as to the legality of the charter, the matter was submitted to the Diocesan Council of the Episcopal Church, in session at Christ Church Cathedral, under the presidency of Bishop Sessums, April 5th, 1894, and the following was the action thereon.

"At the request of the Bishop and of Rev. Arthur Howard Noll, the charter of the Mount Olivet Church was examined, with the view of determing its legality, objection being made: (1) That the charter had not been recorded in the parish where the church was located. (2) That the charter omitted to state the number of years or period it should have existed.

"These and some other minor objections made, were found to be without force, and the charter was held to be in every respect legal and valid.

"The objections stated were founded upon the requirements of law, as now existing, but the charter in question was obtained under the provisions of a former law passed by the Legislature of the State of Louisiana April 30, 1847. All the requirements of that Act were complied with, and the registry of the act of incorporation was made in the office of the Secretary of State at the Capital, and no period for its existence was stated because, under that Act, no limitation was placed upon the existence of the charter so granted. Accordingly, under the terms of the Act of 1847, the duration of the charter in question, which had continuance without limit and became perpetual, and inasmuch as contract and property rights have grown up under it, the charter grant and rights thus acquired became irrepealable."

For future preservation, it was deemed best to have the precious long lost paper made one of record in the Mortgage Office of the Parish of Orleans. To do this, it became requisite to take an acknowledgment in due form of the only signature and seal thereon. For that purpose, Judge Charles Gayarre, the eminent historian was visited April 10th, 1894, and to him was submitted for authentication the copy of the act of incorporation he had affixed his official signature thereto the

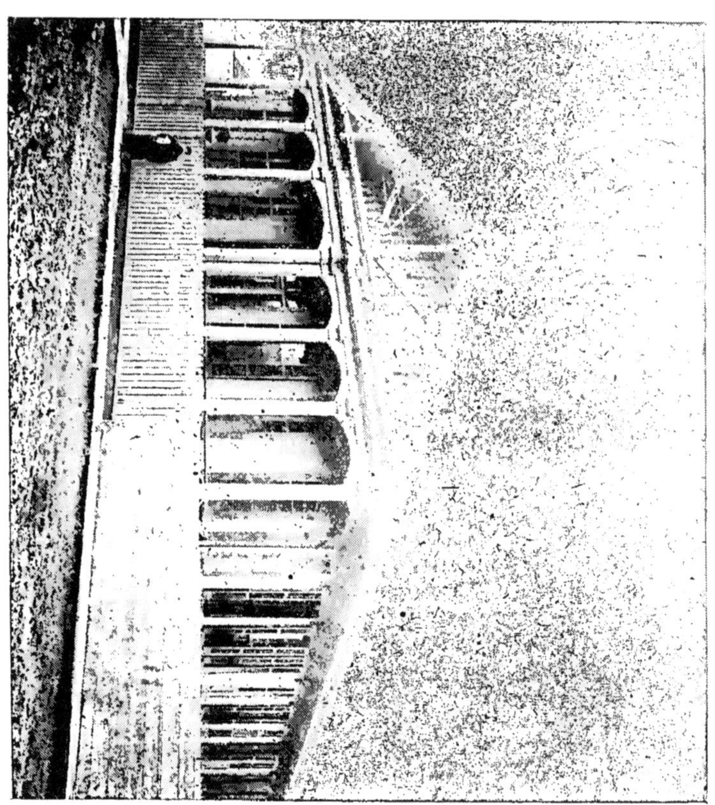

M'DONOGH SCHOOL NO. 5.

1st of January, 1853; over forty-one long years had elapsed, since he had first held he paper in his hand. The recollection of that interview with the old historian, will be one long to be remembered with feeling of love and affection. His intelligent and expressive blue eye, lit up with intellectual light, a face remarkable for its intellectuality.

The act of acknowledgment and the charter was subsequently recorded on the 4th of May, 1894. This was likely the last legal paper examined by the Judge. He died in the ninety-first year of his age, Monday, February 11th, 1895. "As a youth, he consecrated his first ambitions to Louisiaua; through manhood he devoted his pen to her, old, suffering, berift by misfortune of his ancestral heritage, and the fruit of his primes, vigor and industry, he yet stood ever her courageous knight, to defend her. He held her archives, not only in his memory, but in his heart, and while he lived, none dared make public aught about her history, except with his vigilant form in the line of vision."

It can be truthfully asserted, that no other church in the diocese, possessed of charter, has experienced such varied fate, as that, of the one in question. It recalls to memory the vicissitudes and perils of the one granted in the early days of the history of our country. The one issued by a King of England to Connecticut, in colonial times, which during 1687, was hid for safe keeping at Hartford, in the hollow of a venerable oak, which afterwards remained famous as the old Charter Oak for more than a century.

Rev. Mr. Dunn, officiated at one time, he was succeeded by the Rev. Charles V. Hilton, but no service was permitted there during Butler's REGIME, so the building was closed quite a while, unless prayers were voiced by the rector, for the President of the United States, Mr. Hilton's successors were Revs. William Leacock, Alex. Gordon Bakewell, Edward Fontaine, the latter, the author of "How the World was Peopled," published in 1872, and "Science of Hydraulic Engineering," published by the national government at their expense in 1870. A wonderful and talented man he was in every respect. His son, Lamar, was the author of that beautiful war poem. "All quiet along the Potomac to-night." Albert Wilson Starbuck was clerk of the vestry for quite a while, during 1870-73 he revised all the records of the parish from their chaotic state to one of perfection and models for his successor in office. Mr. Starbuck died on the steamship New Orleans, on Sunday, June 29th, 1873, and was buried at sea. He was a giant in statute, mind and intellect of equal magnitude a true friend. In truth may it be said he possessed "A combination and a form indeed, where every god did seem to set his seal, to give the world assurance of a man." Revs. J. F. Girault, Wm. C. McCracken and C. S. Hedges, in turn were succeded by Arthur Howard Noll, a most energetic churchman, to whose persevering work the fine edifice will ever prove a monument. The present rector is a sterling young minister, Rev. Jesse S. Moore, lately ordained, who is accomplishing much good. Charles H. Brownlee is the treasurer of the vestry.

Church of the Holy Name of Mary.

Successor to St. Bartholomew's Church, is situated on Verret between Alix and Evelina streets, and evidences the activity and power of the Catholic Church in Algiers, and the solidity and splendor of its institutions and of its vast importance as

an element in the complex life of the town; with its handsome grounds, and hall occupies nearly all of the block in that section. The Convent and Sisters School is in the adjoining block.

The material of the vast structure is of brick and cement arches. The style is lofty and imposing. Exteriorly the building is impressive and solemn, the tower with clock and spire, massive lofty and majestic, indeed.

In grave and quiet grandeur, the inside of the church with its noble colums is in perfect accord with its outward appearance; the altars and their appointments being rich and elegant. The interior is adorned with French stained glass, masterly altars, and many other treasures of art, all characterized by simplicity, dignity, massiveness and vast size, with electric lights, and a large seating capacity.

The St. Mary's Catholic Club have an elegant hall upon the adjoining corner, with billiards, and stage appurtenance, which is an attractive rendevous for the many members of the club who nightly assemble there. The place is one of many a social gathering, for concerts and kindred entertainments of a pleasing nature.

The grounds adjoining the church are handsomely laid out in serpentine walks with parterres of flowers and shrubbery blooming and blossoming at every turn with artistic design; all the handiwork of the reverend fathers who delight in the labor. Father Gibbons being the GENIE who supervises all, and there passing many a pleasant hour. The property stands registered as belonging to the "Father of the Society of Mary."

The Methodist Episcopal Church.

Of which Rev. Wynn is pastor, has been located for many years upon the corner of Lavergne and Delaronde streets. The congregation is quite a large one, and much good results from the earnest workings of its members. The old building was erected in ANTE BELLUM times, but active steps are now in progress for the demolition of the building and the speedy erection of an edifice more suitable for the convenience of the members, and the progress existing in the immediate and surrounding sections.

The German Evangical Lutheran Trinity Congregation Church is situated on Olivier, corner of Evelina streets. The building is a frame one, with steeple small, but extremely neat and pretty in design. The corporation is chartered, under date of 19th October, 1875. Many of our German citizens worship there, and take a deep and active interest in its welfare and progress.

Colored Churches.

There are many throughout the District. Several of the buildings of worship are really handsome and commodious, and reflect much credit for the taste and ornamental design exhibited in their construction by their various congregations. Beautiful Zion, Mount Pilgrim and St. Mark, are all duly chartered corporations.

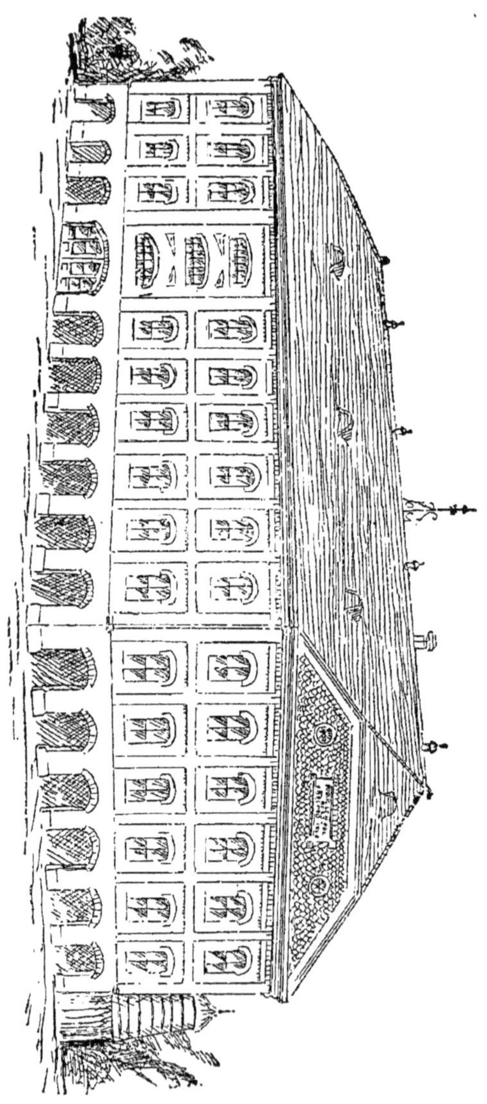

BELLEVILLE SCHOOL.

The Alexander Memorial Library.

THE Alexander Memorial Library, founded by the Faithful Circle of Kings' Daughters in memory of the young hero, Wm. Alexander, who sacrificed his life while endeavoring to save hundreds from the destruction of an incoming train. Mr. Alexander was the favorite son of Mrs. E. M. Hudson, President of the Circle.

After seven years of fortunate existence as an organization, we come together again to celebrate the beginning of a new year of work, and to learn from a review of past endeavors how we shall exert the greatest directing power for good in the future. It is pleasant to note that the influence of the Alexander Library has gone far beyond its success has encouraged the establishment of free reading-rooms in in other localities. There is to be said of all work that is educational, whether it be exerted by mean of public schools or of public libraries, that it is almost impossible to estimate its potency to mold public sentiment or character. Broader views and nobler purposes, higher ideas of life, are imperceptibly installed through these channels. It goes without saying that every community must welcome the establishment of these great factors towards human progress in its midst.

The growth in popularity of the Alexander Library, in the town of Algiers, otherwise known as the Fifth District of New Orleans, has been gradual, but steady, until it has now become a part of the daily life of the people. The past has shown a constant increase in the number of readers, which has necessitated a demand for more room. The Crescent Lodge of Knights of Pythias, with their usual kindness, met this demand by granting a larger allowance of space to the library.

The beginning of the year 1895 finds the library in a good condition, and with all its most urgent needs satisfied. The room has been enlarged, there is more space for the books, more stable accommondation for the periodicals, better light and greater seating capacity for the readers. Through the generosity of sympathizing friends, new books and new periodicals have constantly been added to the fresh reading matter. The liberality of the press has been great and constant. All the large daily newspapers of New Orleans and the Democrat and Herald of Algiers are donated, and their columns are open to any communications tending to attract or stimulate interest in the work. The pen has proved very mighty in this good cause.

The Faithful Circle is glad of an opportunity to thank our home newspapers publicly for their past kindnesses.

Several of the gentlemen of Algiers have been most helpful and encouraging in this enterprise. The protection given the library by the Crescent Lodge, Knights of Pythias, has been of immense value, and the donation of electric lights for the room, a great saving of expense.

CAPTAIN THOS. PICKLES, FERRY LESSEE.

Mr. and Mrs. J. C. Mathewes have been extremely active in their aid to the library, and were most liberal in their donations. The citizens of Algiers have thus shown their appreciation of the fact that anything which tends to the advancement of learning, or a familiarity with things beautiful, is broadening and uplifting; that it means progress and better citizenship for the community.

A free library, through its books and the somtimes exquisite engravings of its periodicals, has an opportunity to gain the popular taste and give it an impulse in the right direction. And this good the Alexander Library seems to be gradually accomplishing. There is no doubt that it is doing a great deal in the way of forming an intelligent reading public, as evidenced by the class of books and periodicals which are asked for by the readers. Magazines relating to certain branches of science and to the mechanic arts are most in demand.

The possibilities of this library are very great, representing, as it does, the only public source of intel ectual recreation or growth in a town of about 16,000 inhabitants, which is separated by a broad river from the libraries, theatres and lecture halls of New Orleans. The members of the Faithful Circle have felt an earnest wish to meet the wants, by means of night classes, of those habitues of the library who desire special training in drawing, in applied sciences and the mechanical trades, but a night school would require more room than is at present at their disposal. With donations of money from sympathizers, with a large membership in the circle, all this and more can be accomplished. The sum of $50, generously given by Miss Annie Howard, as a necleus towards a building fund, now lies in bank awaiting donations from other hands.

The success of the Alexander Library is mainly due to two causes; first the great need of such an institution in the community in which it is placed, and next the intelligent, earnest efforts made by the band of women who are deservedly called "The Faithful Circle." The work of this circle seems to be animated by a broad sprit of love for humanity, by a deep sense of the meaning of its mission, which makes it untiring in its endeavor to solve some of the industrial and educational problems of the nineteenth century.

FELIX BORNE, POLICE COMMISSIONER.

The Embers.

BY MRS. JOSEPHINE HASAM.

Slow over the embers my weary feet
  Go wandering dreamily here and there.
I designate neither corner nor street,
  Homes, one field of cinders, all bare.
Oh, desolation! I fitly exclaim,
  Viewing the wreck, o'er the merciless flame.

Once where I tread, bloomed meadows so green,
  In my girlhood days, what memories abound,
For many and sad the changes I've seen.
  Above this blackened and fire-scathed ground,
There four-leaved clovers plucked, playmates and I,
  When youths fleeting years sped merrily by.

Don't think I am crazed, that I took no repose,
  But stood with the crowd through that fiery night,
And wept not! The Phœnix from ashes arose.
  Look about! There builds in the morning light,
Through the smoke of our ruins yon rising cloud rolls,
  Those "mansions" our Father prepares for our soul.

These are "joys of this earth." There no parting or grief,
  Nor waves overwhelm; no whirlwinds destroy:
No fire can scathe. Life torture is brief,
  To the length that eternity gives us of joy.
Oh "sackcloth and ashes" be mine upon earth,
  Till Phœnix like rises that heavenly birth.

L. J. PETERSON, FIRE COMMISSIONER.

The Algiers Fire.

DESTITUTION, devastation and desolation followed in the wake of the terrible fire which swept over the central portion of Algiers October 20th, 1895. Nine and a half squares of ground were in ashes, and about twenty acres of a forest of chimneys standing, in all their nakedness, gaunt reminders of what had been the center of a thriving and populous community. It was calculated that there were about 200 houses burned, and, with the furniture and with the personal effects which were consumed, the total loss footed up the enormous sum of $600,000.

The fire started as above stated, at 12:45 a. m., in the two-story frame tenement known as the "Old Rookery." It had its origin in the second house from the corner of Bermuda street, on Morgon street, occupied by Paul Bouffia, an Italian who kept a small fruit stand there. The building was occupied by over a dozen families, and some of these had narrow escapes, though all got out safely. As soon as it was discovered, an alarm was turned in, but a high northeast wind was blowing, and fanned the flames into a seething mass, which soon enveloped the entire building.

When the alarm was sent in, the three steam engines and truck of Algiers promptly responded. One engine took up a position on the landing of the Canal Street Ferry, the second at a water well on the corner of Morgan and Seguin streets, while the third was located at the well at the corner Bermuda and Morgan streets. The truck was in front of the building in which the fire originated. Chief Engineer Daly was on hand and instructed the men. For a short time it looked very much like the fire would be confined to this building, but as the wells were emptied of water in the short space of half an hour, the one stream from the engine on the ferry landing could not hold it in check.

The flames then communicated to the adjoining buildings in all directions, and not until the row of houses on both sides of Bermuda street and on one side of Morgan street were in flames did Chief Daly call for assistance from the City proper. It required almost an hour before the City engines could reach the town, by which time the flames had leaped across the street and were consuming the entire square in which the Court House and the Eight Precinct Station were located. When the engines arrived under command of Chief O'Connor, they were all stationed along the levee and drew water from the river.

It is a fact which cannot be contradicted, that if the wind had not changed, the flames would never have been gotten under control until the whole town had been wiped out.

When the house occupied by Paul Bouffia was burning fiercely, in the rear, a report flashed through the crowd that an old woman, who occupied the second floor, was up-stairs and probably overcome with the smoke. James Reynolds, Clerk of the Eight Precinct Police Station, volunteered to rescue her, and he did so by rushing up to the second floor and soon after came out of the burning build-

W. H. Riley M.D.

ing with o'd Mrs. McGinnis in his arms. She had been overcome by the smoke and would have perished in the flames had she not been rescused promptly.

The flames ate their way up Bermuda street and consumed a number of cottages there, and then leaped across the street, attacking the little cottage occupied by Clerk James Reynolds. By this time the community had become aroused to the danger which threated them, and all living in that neighborhood began taking their furniture and valuables out of their houses, and the bulk of this was placed in the yard and corridors of the Court House. This was considered safe, as it was not believed that the flames would succeed in reaching the historic pile. By the brilliant light which the conflagration sent up, illuminating the entire town, the terror-stricken people worked with a will, finding willing helpers, in their more fortunate neighbors, they soon succeeded in storing old stuff in the corriders of the Court House.

But the fury of the flames was far from appeased. Onward and onward they crept, until the entire center of the square, in the rear of the Court House was a veritable inferno. One by one the houses caught, and almost in less time than it takes to tell, handsome little dwellings were reduced to heaps of smoldering ruins. Nearer and nearer came the fire to the Court House. Everybody then began to realized the danger they were in if this was allowed to catch. The little two-story tenement in the rear yard of the station, which was formery the plantation quarters of the darkies who worked for Duverje, caught but a score of hands were soon at work trying to quench the little tongues of flame which sprang up here and there on the shingle roof. A stream of hose was directed on it, and a whole cistern of water was poured on it by the bucketful, but all effort was in vain. In ten minutes it was a heap of burning debris, and the workers directed their attention to the Court House, which had already caught. A little double cottage next to it was sending up great tongues of flame, which had ignited the roof and wood work on the gallery, and the slate roof of the Court House acted as a slight check. The flames ate their way beneath the slate, on the rafters and joists, and it was soon a seething mass. So confident was everyone that this building could be saved, that they hesitated to remove their furniture and their goods which they had stored therein, until the last moment, and then it was too late. The Court records were also left to the last minute and the bulk of these also went up in smoke. All the old records of the City Court, the records of births, marriages and deaths before the Board of Health took charge of that work, and all but two books of the Recorder's Court were burned. The employes of the Police Station, however, were more fortunate and managed to save every scrap of paper belonging to their department. When the old roof fell in it sent up a shower of sparks and chunks of burning wood, which, while it formed a pretty sight, was disastrous to the houses which were to the windward. But the massive brick walls served one good purpose, and that was to save the buildings on the river side.

In the meantime the City engines had arrived, and, with Chief O'Connor in control, concerted efforts were put into force to check the flames, but they were as naught against the terrible gale which was blowing. Chief of Police Gaster also arrived, with Mayor Fitzpatrick, and, with an additional force of police and firemen, they set to work assisting the unfortunates who were domiciled in the path of the raging element. The department was sadly handicapped by a lack of hose and water, as it had to be pumped all the way from the river in relays.

MANUEL ABASCAL.

The flames even ate their way in the face of the wind and burned out almost the entire square in which the fire originated. It leaped over to the next square, bounded by Lavergne, Delaronde, Bermuda and Pelican, and, in the course of half an hour, had wiped off all but three buildings, and the rear of these were scorched. When it was seen that the flames were likely to reach out in this direction, down the river, steam was started in the saw mill of Hotard & Lawton, and, with a lead of 1300 feet of hose, a stream was kept constantly playing on the houses fronting on Lavergne street by the fire brigade of the mill. There is no doubt in the world that they prevented the fire from crossing that street, and thus saved a vast amount of property from destruction. There was not a single fire engine in this vicinity, which seemed to be abandoned to its fate, and while the fire was prevented from crossing Lavergne street, it forged ahead, driven by furious winds towards Bermuda and Seguin streets, and, unresisted, ate its way in a course almost parallel with the river, until it had practically burned itself out.

The entire area covered by the fire looked like a veritable inferno, continually spreading out, leaping from one street to another almost before the people in that square knew that it was there. Sparks lighting on the roofs of houses, driven thither by the wind, would ignite, and soon half a dozen houses would begin to burn in a square at one time. Some efforts were made to guard against these sparks by people, who stationed themselves, with buckets of water on shingled-roofed dwellings, waiting for the little tongues of flame to shoot up, when they would be quenched, but while the volunteer was engaged in putting this flame out another would gain such headway on him that he would have to scamper down with all haste to save himself from the fire, which spread with great rapidity. The firemen would no sooner get a line of hose fixed on a street and start to fight the fire from the windward, when the flames would drive them away, and in several instances large sections of hose were burned and melted so as to be rendered useless. People moving their furniture from houses in danger would, with great difficulty, and the aid of volunteers, succeeded in getting it a block away, and in apparent safety, when they would find that all their labor was in vain, as the flames would swoop down on that square, and the whole thing would become a seething furnace in no time. Many persons lost their furniture, which they had saved from burning houses, in this manner.

When the flames had eaten their way to the river front above the Grand Isle Depot the sight presented was one long to be remembered, both by the poor unfortunates who had been driven out of their homes by the relentless element and by the spectors who gazed in awe on the terrible havoc being wrought. Two leads of hose were being operated by the Southern Pacific Tug El Chico and the Corsair, and they did effective work in checking the flames. Mayor Fitzpatrick, who is an old volunteer fireman, made good use of his experience as a foreman of No. 13, and with an overcoat drawn up over his ears to protect him from the showers of sparks which were falling around like a hail of fire, he directing operations in that vicinity with good results. By the most persistent work and with great difficulty the fire was checked at Alix street, though it was necessary to continue playing the hose on the houses on the opposite side of the street to prevent the buildings from catching fire from the heat.

About 5 o'clock, when the fireman were directing their energies in this locality, which was the first real effort made with any degree of success at checking the fire's headway, sparks fell on the roof of a coal office belonging to W. G. Coyle &

F. Henning

Co., about a thousand yards up the river, and soon that building was a mass of flames. Around here were a number of coal barges and other property, and it looked as if a serious conflagration would break out here, but the Tug Wilmot was put into service and prevented the fire from spreading.

As daylight dawned the brilliancy of the spectacle became more subdued, and with the advance of the successful efforts of the fire fighters the flames died out gradually until by noon only here and there in the vast forest of gaunt and grim chimneys little tongues of fire would shoot up from the heaps of smoking debris, seemingly defiant to the last. All day a huge gray cloud floated many miles in the air above the town, slowly moving away and being absorbed into the atmosphere, until when night fell again over the scence of desolation it had vanished from view.

Mr. C. Uncas Lewis made a diagram of the burned section. Mr. Lewis made an estimate of the number of houses which had been burned, and it foots up a total of 193. He estimates the loss on buildings at $300,000, and on personal property and furniture at $100,000, making a total of $400,000.

To provide for the unfortunate people rendered homeless by the fire was a serious question which rose up before the people of Algiers that Sunday morning. A thousand or more people had to be provided with shelter of some kind, and where temporary homes could be found for them was a question indeed hard to solve. Some families were housed in McDonogh School No. 4, others in the Masonic, Pythian and Eureka Halls. Every house which was vacant, every room which was for rent was quickly taken, and every person was provided with temporary quarters. The old Planters' Oil Works, at the corner of Belleville and Paterson, was also utilized as shelter for the homeless.

While the destruction of property was enormous, and to be deplored, it is gratifying that not one life was lost nor any one injured. Not so much as a horse was burned.

Hundreds upon hundreds of people crossed to Algiers on the Canal and St. Ann street ferries. The intelligence of the terrible conflagration in Algiers was not made known fully to the morning paper readers, for the fire continued to burn long after the papers were on the streets. Later in the day the full news was given to the residents of the city, and the ferries made trips as fast as they could cross, tie up and get another human cargo.

The terrors, the agonies, the suspense that attended the conflagration were not made as manifest to the visitors as they were to the persons on the scene. The pictures presented to the spectators during the mad sweep of flames are indescribable. Aged women could be described rushing along from one place to another, through smoke-filled streets, carrying something from a doomed building. They stumbled and fell. Little children with arms full of something or other weighted down, dove around corners to get out of the smoke and flame, for they really in many instances ran between burning buildings. They deposited their burdens and going back, secured another armful. Little girls, mothers, husbands, sons, in and out of different streets, did the same thing, and many of these having made a storehouse of the banquette, saw big live coals of fire drop into the bedding stored there and the next thing they were consumed Women sat on their galleries and waited for the fire to get upon them before they would relinquish the place they called home and loved with all of a woman's devotion. Others, insured, stood before the closed doors and waited until the all-consuming flames had taken hold. There

Hennings

were some men who worked as they never had before in efforts to help poor wome remove their household effects and there were other men who stood about and looked on women and young girls freighted down with burdens and offered no assistance. Some of the men folks at one end of the town were working with a will to help save household effects of friends and in the morning they found they were burned out themselves. Many were under the impression that the fire was sweeping from the corner of Bermuda and Morgan streets in a northwesterly direction to the river front, while it was eating to the right left and everywhere.

Even while the flames were licking the sides of the court building and playing with the telephone wires, the news was being sent along and was sent until the exchange said the wires were grounded, and then the fire had gotten through the wire and the court was in flames.

Judge Sam Levy proved himself a good man in an emergency. Seeing that the fire was about to assume big proportions he went to Gouldsboro on a mule and summoned the engine from there.

Committee Clerk of the City Council Martin Behrman, who resides in Algiers, a little beyond the range of the fire, saw the necessity of immediate relief for the people and started out on a canvas of his own for subscriptions.

The man with the camera was one of the early morning visitors on the scene He got in the burned district and got views from every quarter. He went into the different squares and really took the situation from all points.

Late in the evening it was difficult to get around the burned quarter on the sidewalks. The crowd from the city was big enough to make something of a continuous moving procession. Many of this crowd interrogated the unfortunates and learned for themselves the true nature of the distress they were in. And it may be said that many a dollar was slipped into the hand of a fire-sufferer. It goes to show that a person brought face to face with a calamity is touched to the extent of contributing as becomes the man who is human.

Mayor Fitzpatrick got on the scene when the fire was at its worst. He found a position on the river front and took an active hand in the direction of the men, making a good assistant to Chief O'Connor. He got the men to the front of the fire, where they should have been earlier in the action, and though Alix street was beginning to take, the firemen got behind shutters torn from buildings and fought the flames to a finish right there. Chief O'Connor and the mayor remained until all danger was past.

Judge Seymour, who presides at the Third City Court, was in Atlanta, Ga. All of the old marriage licenses and records of the court were lost in the fire.

When the fire was raging in its fiercest in the morning, the wind was blowing a cyclone. The dust on the street was parched and this was blown in a person's face, and it cut and burned dreadfully. The eyes were especially effected by the dust. This wind floated quarter shingles through the air.

One of these things which even a man with little of the finer feelings can pass unnoticed was the spectacle presented at the inner edge of the banquette near the corner of Seguin and Alix streets. When the flames had died away in this section and the sidewalk was accessible, the linemen putting up the new electric wires found the bodies of two dogs that had been burned to a crisp. They were cuddled together, and, judging from the position in which they were found, had crawled under the front stoop and shoved their noses to an opening that must have been in the bottom of the step to breathe. And it was here they were cremated, as close

together as they could get. The position in which they were found told the story as well as if the death had been witnessed. The linemen out of the very feeling that comes to men at such a time, covered the poor brutes where they were. The woman who lived on the premises told the men that the dogs had awakened her, and she did all in her power to get them out of the place, but they were frightened and ran under the stoop and could not be dragged out.

The fire was a good thing for the Algiers, McDonoghville and Gretna car line. The residents of Gretna and McDonogh were as anxious to see the sight as the Orleanians, and they took the only street car line on this side of the river. During the progress of the fire the Company was not feeling very good, for the blaze was very close to the stables at one time, and it became necessary to remove the rolling and propelling stock.

The Grand Isle Roundhouse, about 100 yards from the upper end of the fire, and the Office and Freight Shed at the lower end of it, were in eminent danger at one time, but for the good work of the pump that supplied the reservoir, this being situated between both buildings, they would have been destroyed. The reservoir has pipe leads to the Roundhouse and Shed. Hose was attached at each end, and the roofs of both buildings were kept soaked all the time.

Among the Towboats were of great service at the fire were Corsair, Maud Wilmot, El Mozo and Elmer Woods. They took up different positions in the river and gave out leads of hose that were put to good use by the firemen.

Officer Chubbuck, from the City side of the river, detailed to duty at the corner of Bermuda and Alantic avenue, said that he saved a little child from certain cremation. The little one was making her way through an alley on Bermuda near Alix street, and pieces of burning timber were falling about her on all sides. Had she progressed further in the alley, there would be no going beyond except into the flames, so he ran in, grabbed her while the alley was filling with burning brands and rushing out, soaked her in the gutter, thinking she was burning, She got nothing but a soaking.

Charles Featherling, Engineer of the Algiers Saw Mill, remained at the pump that was delivering water on the fire while his own home was being destroyed, and was aware of it all the time. He had no other man to take his place, so he held the fort.

After the fire had burned back to Delaronde street and the houses on the river side were in flames, Mr. Samuel Levy called out the Volunteer Fire Company, which used the old hand pump of Morgan Company No. 4. The volunteers for some time prevented the flames from crossing the street. The pump was subsequently abandoned, however. Four gentlemen happened to come along at this time, and, seeing the apparatus lying idle, and the houses on the Railroad side of the street in danger, they took charge of the fire fighter and fought the flames until the heat became too intense to remain any longer. Three of them would do the pumping while the fourth held the nozzle and kept the front of the houses and roofs damp, which prevented them from catching fire.

In the morning two young ladies of Algiers, Misses Flora Hurlbet and M. Skelly, gained for themselves the admiration of many by their prompt realization of the situation and their prompt response. They saw that the firemen and citizens who for the time being had been made firemen in their labors fighting the flames were being tired and exhausted, and hastily arranging a convenient table made for them an abundance of coffee, which with short lunches were supplied to

S. Daniels
P S Lawton
A E Holand

the men at work. This was very much appreciated by the firemen, for theirs was an arduous and tiresome, as well as an exhausting task.

Along the river front lived the poorer people, those who could afford only rented houses, and possessing barely a set of furniture, Italians, negroes and humble workers of all classes. These poor people, as soon as they saw that their homes were destined to be swallowed up in the relentless fires, rapidly carried their effects over the embankment, down to the water's edge, and there deposited them on the batture.

All along the batture for a distance of nearly a mile from the Wood's docks, which are located eight or ten blocks above the Grand Isle Depot, to the Canal Street Ferry Landing, the northern border of the fire limit, the batture was filled with men, woman and children.

Women half-clad were standing with shawls on their heads watching the smoke curling above the chimney-tops, and dreaming of the morrow. Children, aroused from peaceful slumber in the dead hours of the night, stood crying and sobbing around the feet of distressed and povety-stricken parents. Here and there an old negro woman, her face a degree blacker with dust and ashes, and her clothes barely fastened to her body, stood guard by a small tub of clothes and a few pieces of old chairs. Men stood about on the batture with their wives, moaning the loss of every stick of furniture, and all their clothing, save what could be hastily seized as they were hurried out of a home already fast becoming the food of the hungry flames.

Women with babies upon their breasts sat flat upon the ground and gave their young nourishment. Little bare-headed and bare-footed boys, fatigued and worn out with the excitement of the night, lay sleeping on the grass, and on every side were homeless and suffering people. Th s picture was one long scene of distress, extending for a mile down the river front.

Now and then, as the levee front was traversed, men were found, who, with more pluck, were mending furniture hastily snatched from the flames and getting things ready for home-making again. Many of the men, as soon as they had saved their goods, hastily sought out new homes further back in the city, and were carrying them thither.

The Relief Committee.

The measures for the relief of the destitute were put under way early during the day, and by 4 o'clock in the afternoon, a thoroughly organized and systematic effort was being made for the assistance of the unfortunates who lost their all in the fire. There was fully 100 families who lost everything they possessed, and many others who, while they saved a little furniture, were unable to find a refuge or obtain food.

At an early hour in the morning, a number of the leading citizens of the burg met at the residence of Mr. Martin Behrman, to devise some means of relief. Mr. P. S. Lawton acted as Chairman, and Mr. Behrman occupied the desk. After discussing the situation, it was decided that a Mass Meeting be held at 3 o'clock in the afternoon at the Eureka Hall, and the following call was issued and widely circulated:

M Hambacher
R F Whitmore

"A great calamity has overtaken a portion of our people. A disastrous conflagration, covering an erea of ten squares, has swept out of existence nearly 200 houses, whose occupants, driven in terror and confusion, were powerless, in a great many cases, to save aught but their lives. Numbers of these people have neither food nor shelter, nor the means to procure either. These people are our friends—they are in need—and it is proposed to help them. We, therefore, call upon our more fortunate brethren to meet us at Eureka Hall at 3 o'clock this day (Sunday), and contribute to the full measure of their means. Come one and all, and come prepared to act promptly, as this is one of the cases where giving quickly is giving doubly.

MANUEL ABASCAL,	O. I. McLELLAN,
A. E. HOTARD,	P. S. LAWTON,
F. R. HURLBURT,	MARTIN BEHRMAN,
GEO. W. FOSTER,	PETER CLEMENTS,
FRANK A. DANIELS,	MARK A. MORSE,
T. F. MAHER,	F. C. HENNING,
ARTHUR DUVIC,	T. G. BRIGHAM."

In the meantime lists were gotten up, and quite a large sum collected by the gentlemen who had assembled at the first meeting.

The mass meeting assembled at Eureka Hall shortly after 3 o'clock, and there were fully 200 citizens of the town present. The report had been circulated throughout the town that some action would be taken in regard to a contemplated expulsion of the Italian element of the population, and, while there were a mutterings among some people who took their losses very hard, nothing of the sort developed at the meeting, which was conducted in the most orderly manner, and there was not even the slightest suggestion of such a contemplated action.

When there were a sufficient number of persons in the Hall, comprising all the best element of the people of the burg, several leaders of the movement prevailed on Mayor Fitzpatrick, who was present, to take chair.

Mayor Fitzpatrick called the meeting to order, and as a preliminary statement said that they were assembled to take action and not to express sympathy, therefore, the sooner they got down to work the better it would be for everybody. He then read the call for the meeting, as above, and added that speedy action was the most important object in view. It was a business meeting, and not one of sentiment.

Mr. Martin Behrman moved that an Executive Relief Committee of twenty-one be appointed to take charge of the work of relief. The motion was put and carried without dissent.

Before the gentlemen were named, the Mayor suggested that it would be well to elect a Secretary of the meeting, and this was done by the selection of Mr. Martin Behrman.

A recess of ten minutes was then taken to permit the Mayor to select the Committee. They were then announced as follows:

Peter S. Lawton, Manuel Abascal, Frank A. Daniels, Martin Behrman, T. J. Brigham, R. F. Whitmore, F. R. Hurlburt, Mark A. Morse, Thos. Higgins, Thos. J. Mooney, Peter Clements, Henry Carstens, O. I. McLellan, L. A. Hymel, A. E. Hotard, Frank C. Henning, Max Hambacher, H. L. Sease, Geo. W. Foster, T. F. Turnbull and W. F. Umbach.

A small list of contributions was then read, and then a second recess was taken to allow the collection of additional amounts from the gentlemen in the meeting. This collection resulted in a very marked augmentation of the total.

Mr. Brigham suggested that those who were not able to contribute money be recognized to afford shelter to the homeless. Many persons were able to house one or two families. He had three rooms which were at the disposal of the Committee.

Other gentlemen said that the Eureka Hall, Pythian Hall, McDonogh Schoolhouses and other buildings were at the disposal of the destitute.

Then another recess was taken to receive the contributions, and the Mayor announced the grand total as $7373.

The thanks of the citizens were tendered to Mayor Fitzpatrick despite his protest.

The following resolution was also adopted.

Resolved, That the thanks and appreciation of the citizens of Algiers is hereby expressed to Messrs. Hotard & Lawton, proprietors of the Algiers Saw Mill, for their timely and valuable assistance in preventing the extension of the conflagration over a large territory by furnishing hose and pumps connected with their mill, in use of which the properties of Carstens & Vezien, Abascal and many other residences along Lavergne and other streets were saved from the raging flames.

Be it further resolved, That we recommend to the Board of Underwriters and insurance companies interested, the equipping of said Algiers Saw Mill with a complete set of hose and and necessary appurtenances as a precautionary measure in the future.

The mass meeting then adjourned subject to call, and the executive committee met.

Peter S. Lawton was elected chairman, Martin Behrman secretary and Mark A. Morse treasurer.

It was decided that the full committee be subdivided into four sub-committees of five each to canvass the squares which had been destroyed, and make an immediate report as to the neeessities of the destitute.

The committee then went out to work, after agreeing to meet again at Eureka Hall at 8 o'clock p. m. October 21.

Mayor Fitzpatrick suggested the advisability of issuing an address to the people, explaining the destitution and asking for assistance, which was adopted by the committee.

The following proclamation was issued by Mayor Fitzpatrick :

PROCLAMATION.

To the People of New Orleans:

A committee of representative citizens of the Fifth District of this City have issued a call for relief in behalf of the afflicted people of that section, caused by the disastrous conflagration of Sunday morning. The relief must be had at once to relieve the present suffering.

Appreciating the unbounded charity of the people of New Orleans, and the great and impressing necessity of assisting the great number of deserving people who have been suddenly thrown out of doors by the fire, I issue this call for aid, requesting such assistance in money, food and clothing as may be tendered.

All subscriptions, clothing or provisions will be thankfully received by Mr. Peter Lawton, Chairman Citizens' Committee, Algiers, or at the City Hall, Mayor Office. JOHN FITZPATRICK, Mayor.

The four committees then headed for the police station, where they secured a partial list of the families who were burned out, and then started out to hunt them up, to ascertain their exact needs and provide for them as soon as possible. As there was nearly a thousand dollars collected at the meeting in cash money, the immediate necessities of the destitute were relieved at once.

The people of Algiers who were so fortunate as to escape the conflagration lost no time in manifesting an active sympathy for their suffering and unfortunate neighbors. Indeed, in this respect, the people of Algiers showed remarkable alacrity, sustaining their reputation of being the most charitable people in the city.

These committees were chairmaned by the following gentlemen: Committee No. 1, Frank Daniels; No. 2, R. F. Whitmore; No. 3, Peter Clements; No. 4, F. T. Turnbull. Each of these committees, with the above named chairmen, were composed of prominent gentlemen of Algiers, who went into their work with a will.

After the meeting had accomplished this, an adjournment was taken, and the four committees went about their work of mercy. They spent the rest of the evening in making an inspection of the burned district and getting the needed infor mation.

Then again the meeting reassembled at Eureka Hall, and was called to order. The various chairmen made their reports, giving the names of those in need of relief.

From that period in the cause of charity so urgent, contributions were handed into the Committee with prompt liberality. Among the contributions of special note were: City of New Orleans, through Mayor Fitzpatrick, $5000; Hon. Adolph Meyer, Washington, D. C., $500; Southern Pacific Company, $1000; D. H. Holmes, $300; Thomas Pickles, $500; John Fitzpatrick, $250; O. I. McLellan, $150; Security Brewing Company, $200, through Sam Levy; Southern Telephone Company, $200; Barber Asphalt Company, W. G. Tebault, Geraci & Foto, Manuel Abascal & Bro., George E. Corbett, Eureka Homestead Company, Isadore Newman, Firemen's Building Association, American Brewing Company, Wm. H. Seymour, Atlanta, Ga., thorough Judge Mooney, New Orleans Brewing Association, S. Hernsheim Bros, & Co., L. Fabacher, each, $100; Grand Opera House, $128; colored laborers on wharf Southern Pacific Company, $189; through Times-Democrat, $446; through N. O. Picayune, $964, all of which was most carefully distributed with great prudence.

A large number of citizens, including the members of the Relief Committee, contributed also as their means and circumstances would permit, while others, including the Orphan Asylums and Charitable Associations gave clothing, provisions, drugs and bedding, sent from all portions of the City with free and willing hand in aid of the sufferers, which was gladly received, and prudently distributed among the needy. It was a cause of much regret, however, to note that some who were bound by many ties to the place, from birth or other kindred associations, with abundant means, failed to throw any bread of charity upon the sea of trouble and tribulation existing, upon such a rare occasion in a lifetime. He who gave quickly, gave doubly, in those days of sorrow.

For the members of the Relief Committee, their assistants, and the Chief Magistrates of the City at that epoch, words cannot express what is due them. May the recording angel so High, keep full record of their noble work; a kindly Providence walk unseen by their side in future years to bless and to brighten all their hands dare to do and their hearts dare to hope.

Several meetings were held as occasion required until the final one of Sunday November 10th, 1895, when the last exhibit was presented, showing the total receipt of all funds to that date to have been $15,994.25. The residue remaining was then donated to the kind Sisters of the Convent to dispose of as they might see proper for benevolence in the town.

A meeting was subsequently held the same month and attended by many receipients and beneficiaries of the large fund and goods disiributed. Resolutions of thanks fittingly worded and expressed were submitted by Joseph Hughes, and unanimously adopted, tendering the late Relief Committee heartfelt thanks for all the good they had accomplished in their work of charity.

FINALE.

A few months ago, one walking along the main streets of the town looked across a wide tract of desolute ruins. Heaps of ashes were there, gaunt and tottering chimneys and fire-blasted trees. All over the town homeless and hopeless families were crowded into the temporary quarters with the remnant of their household goods gathered about them.

Let the visitor make the same journey now. The way will be long, pretty streets, with new and buautiful homes lined up on either side. Looking at those houses with their Schillinger walks, neat iron fences and the flower beds, gay with flowers, Morgan street paved for nearly a mile with vitrified bricks upon concrete foundation. The new viaduct looming up in the distance, near by the tall Waterworks reservoir with many other improvements. The same sky is overhead, the same earth beneath, the same sun shines as brightly now as some months ago, but a walk now along those attractive streets make it difficult to realize that this was the same so lately in ashes and ruins. May universal peace and happiness in all future years sway their sceptre over this happy, busy town.

A Executive Order Issued by Governor Carondelet.

An order of the olden times, issued by Francois Louis Hector Baron de Carondelet, (Spanish Governor of the Province of Louisiana,) contributed by a lady to the Story of Algiers :

"New Orleans, 30 June, 1796.

The persons named Laurent, Petit, Etienne and LeGrand, will not interfere with, or disturb the person named Barthelemy Blue, in the possession of the Island at Timbalier, which was given to him by decree of the Government.

LeBaron de Carondelet."

The story is ended. The task is done.

[*FINIS.*]

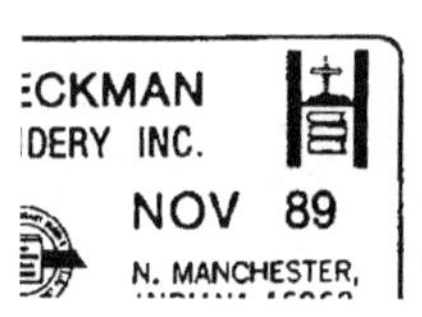

CPSIA information can be obtained
at www.ICGtesting.com
Printed in the USA
BVHW041322130919
558397BV00005B/59/P

9 780342 471409